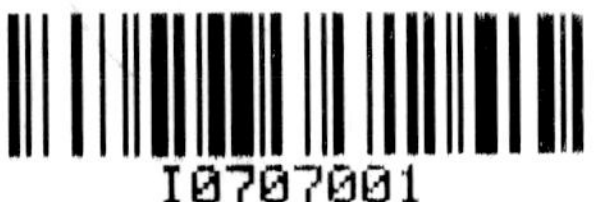

For the little dreamers and artists, may this book fill your world with joy, imagination, and endless colors.

Carlos Gabriel

2024

Test Color Page

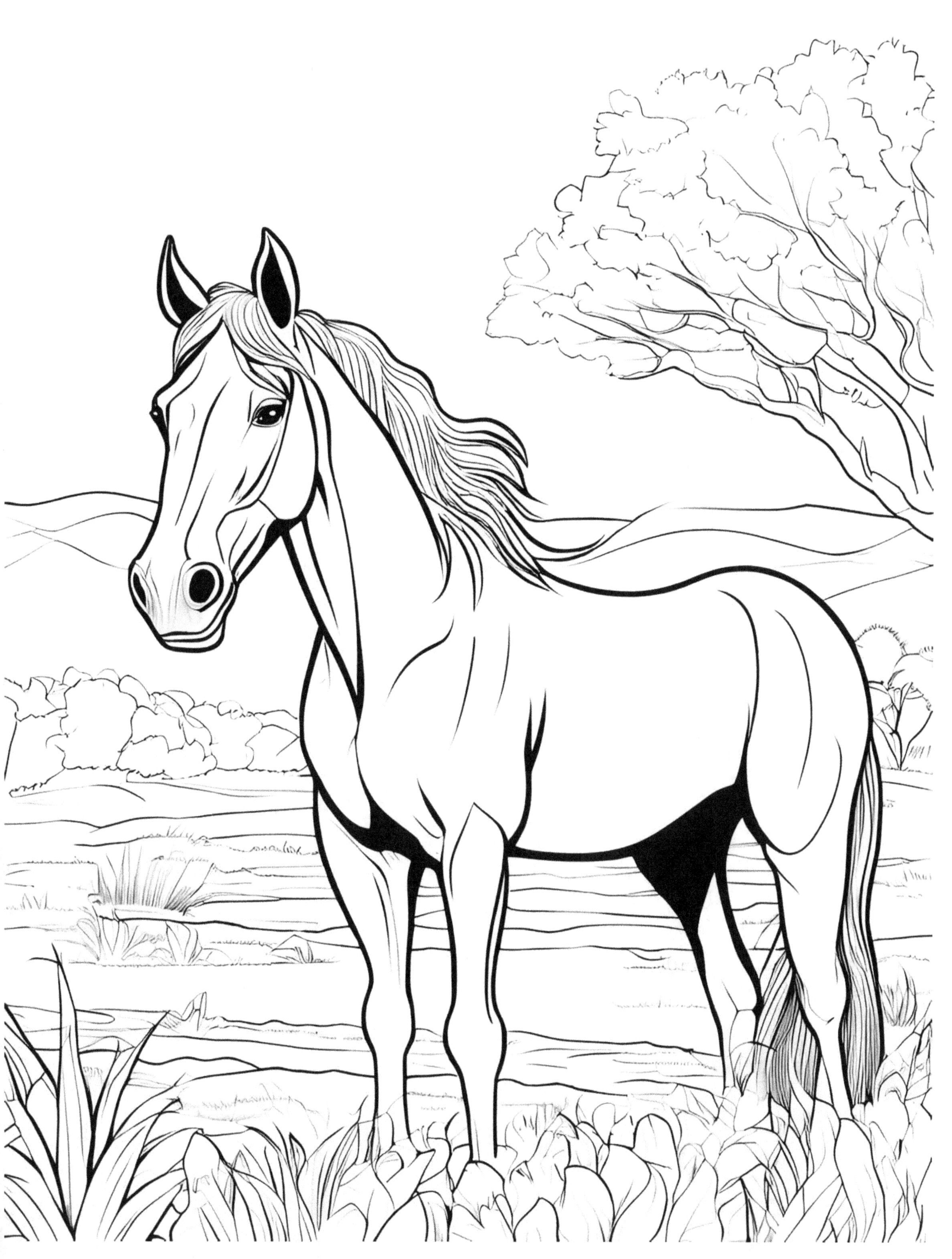

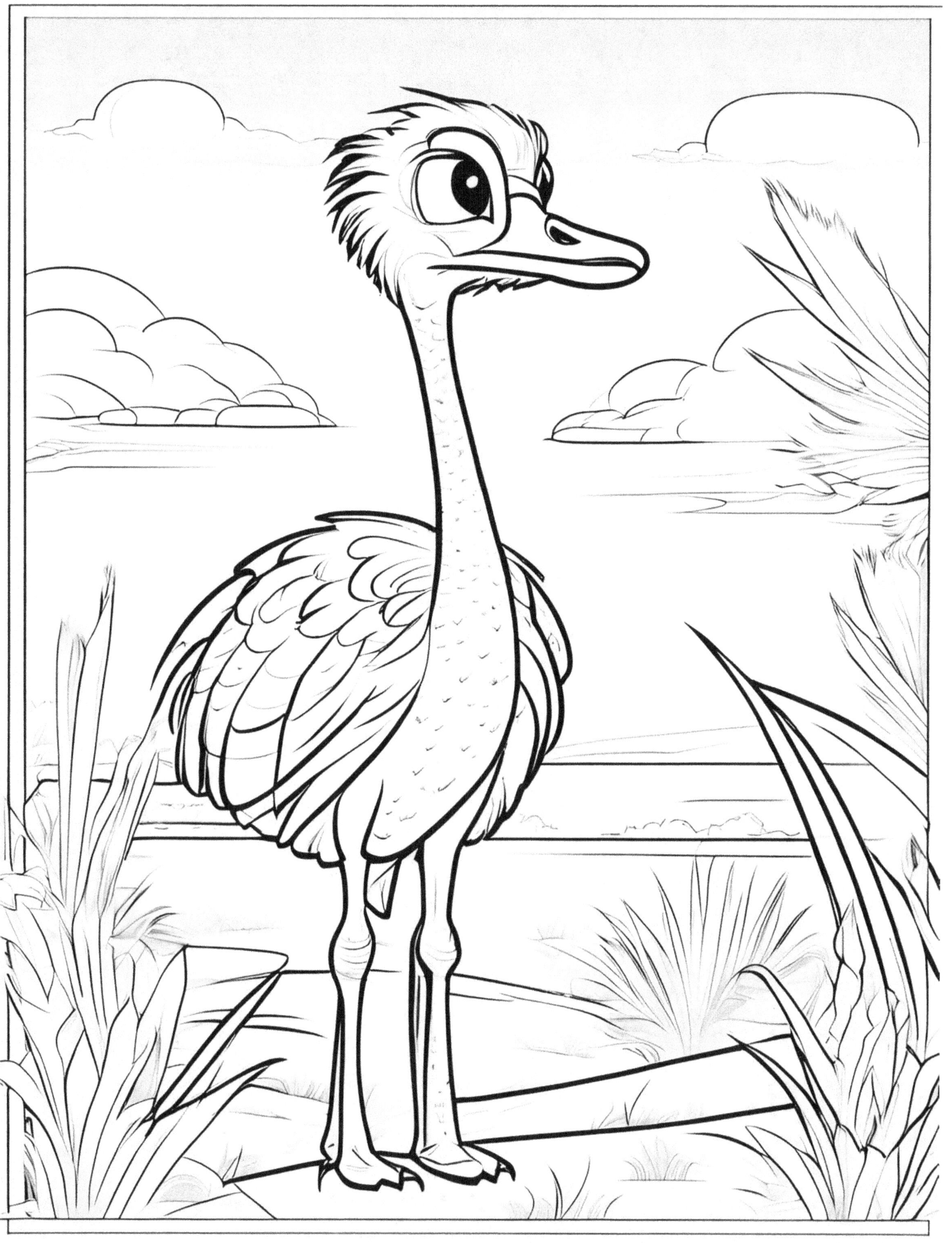

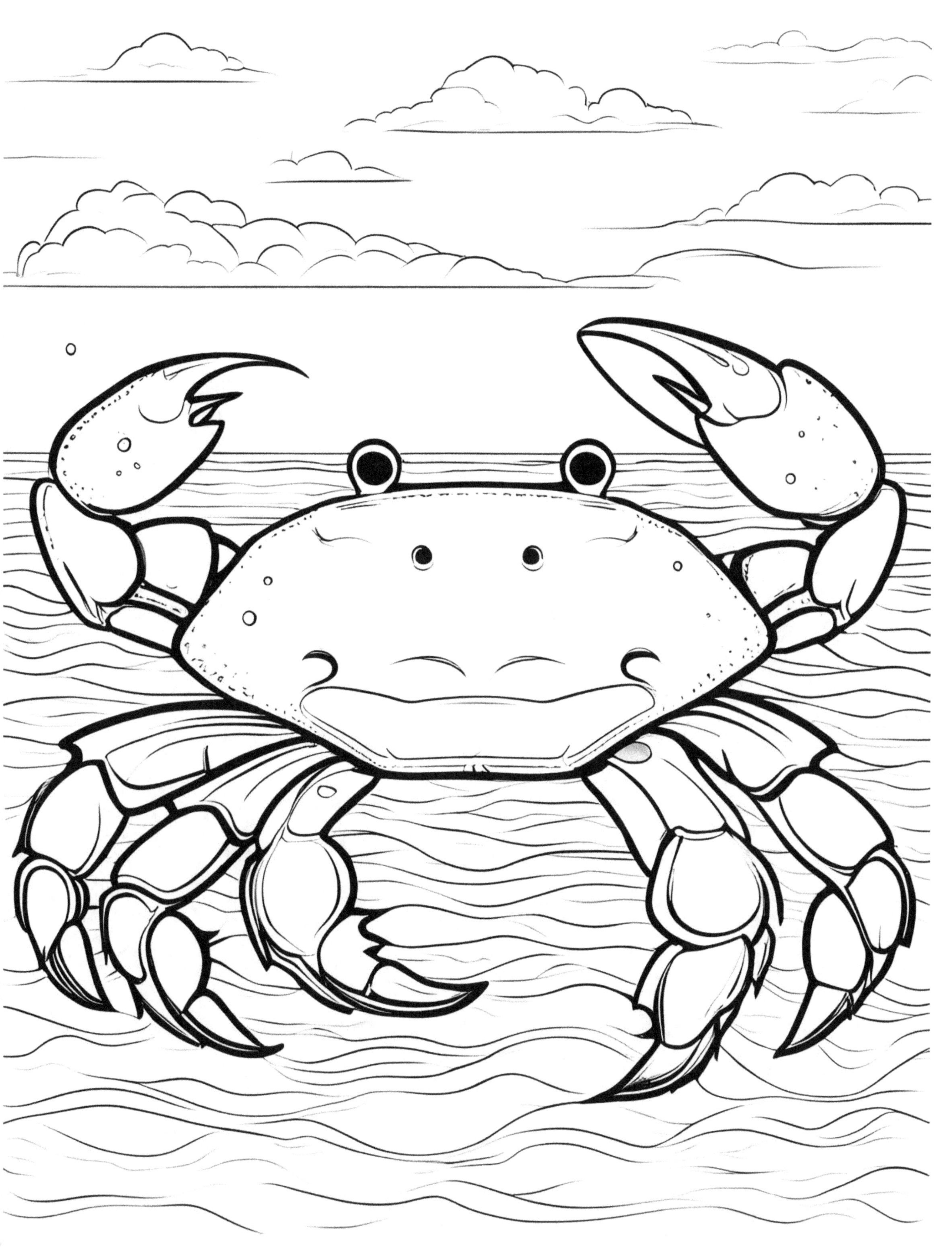

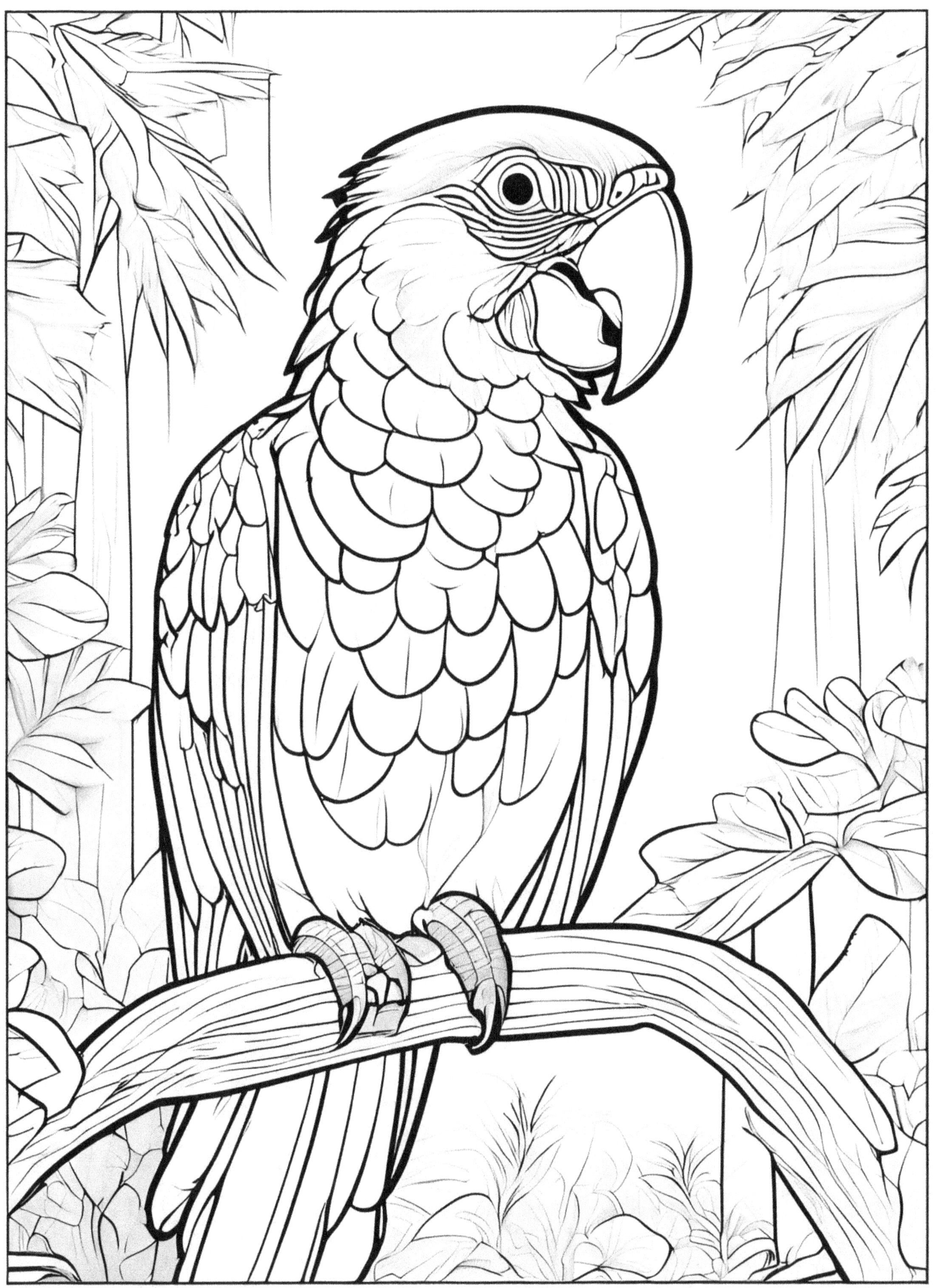

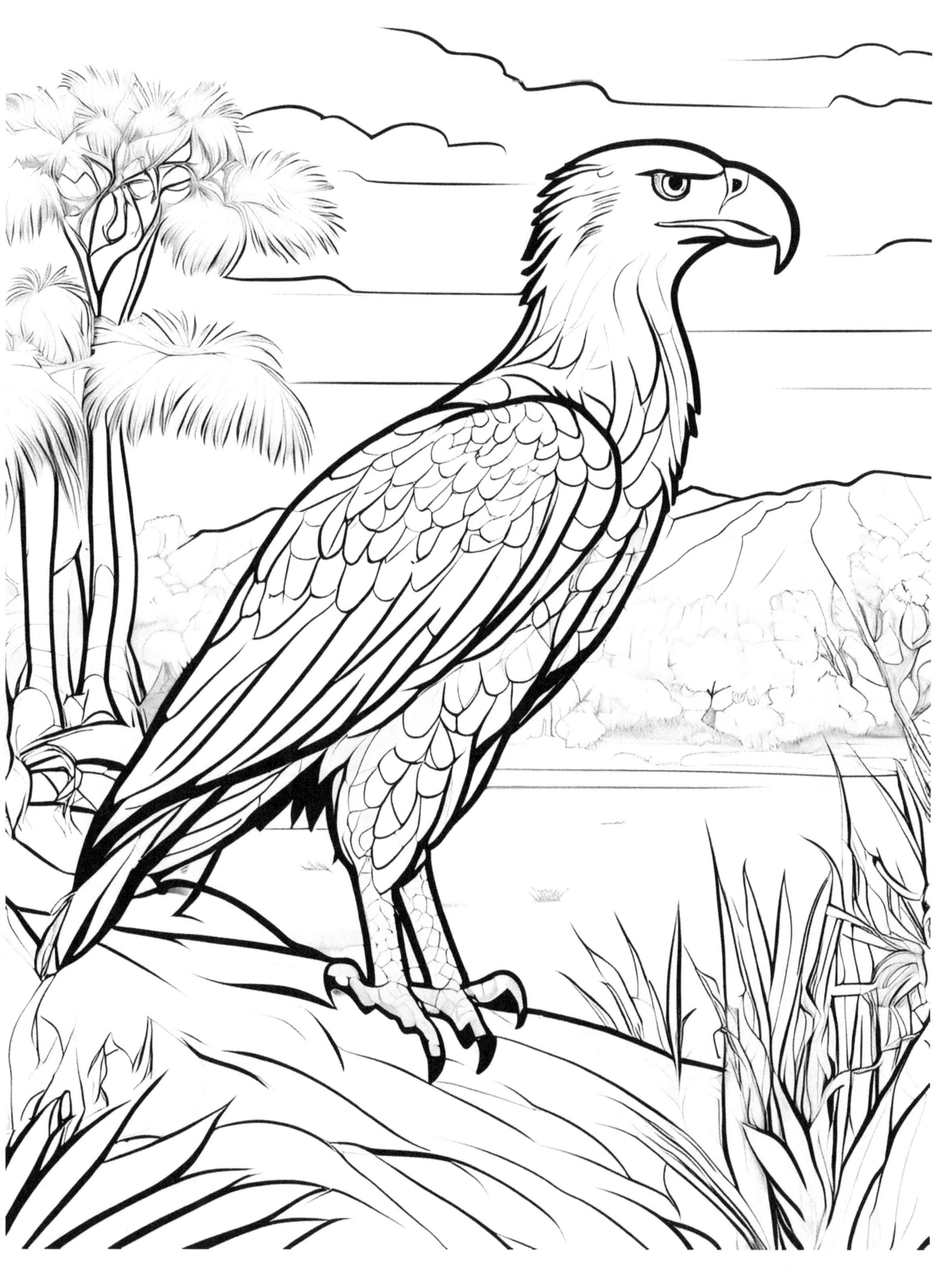

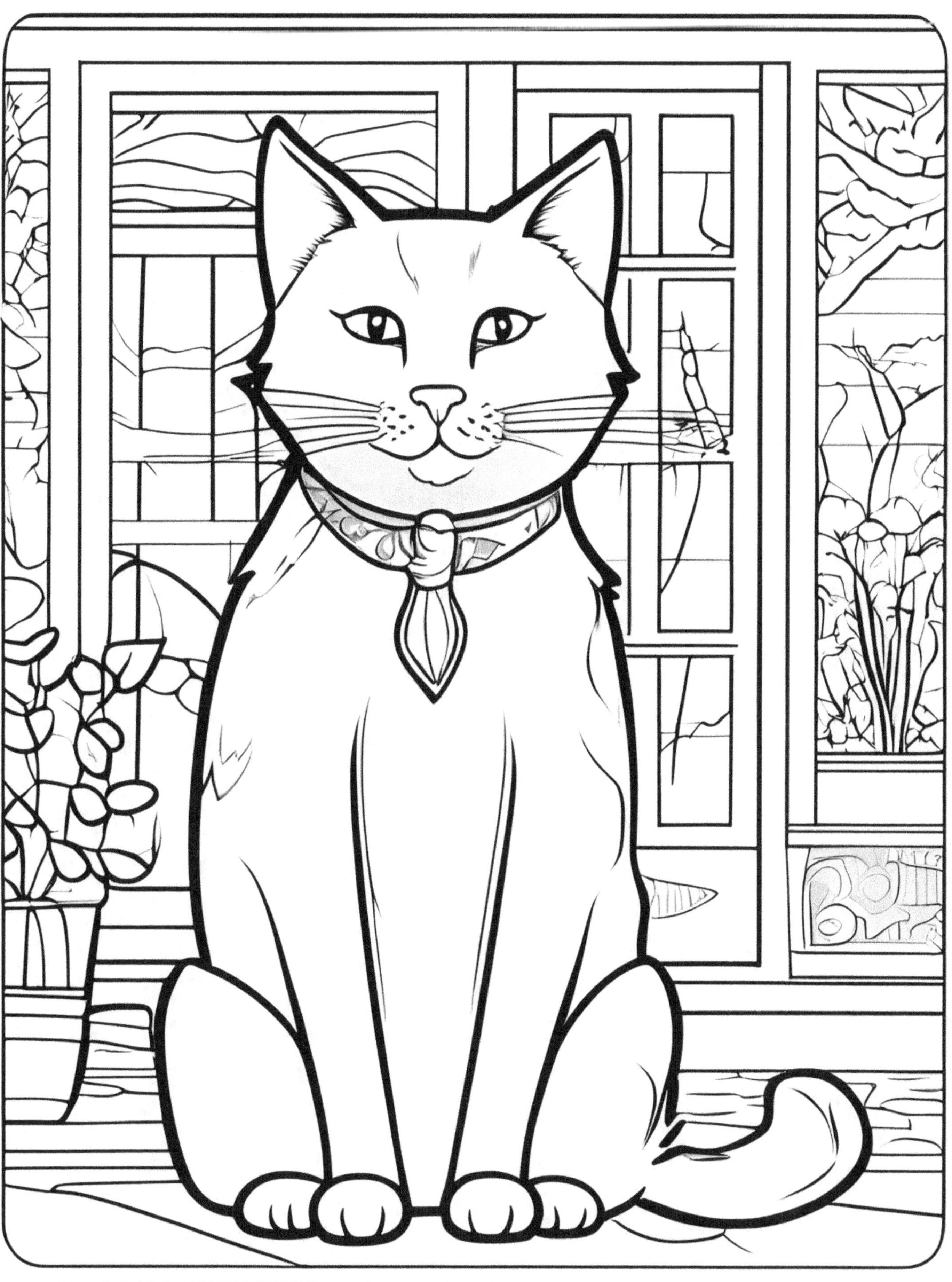

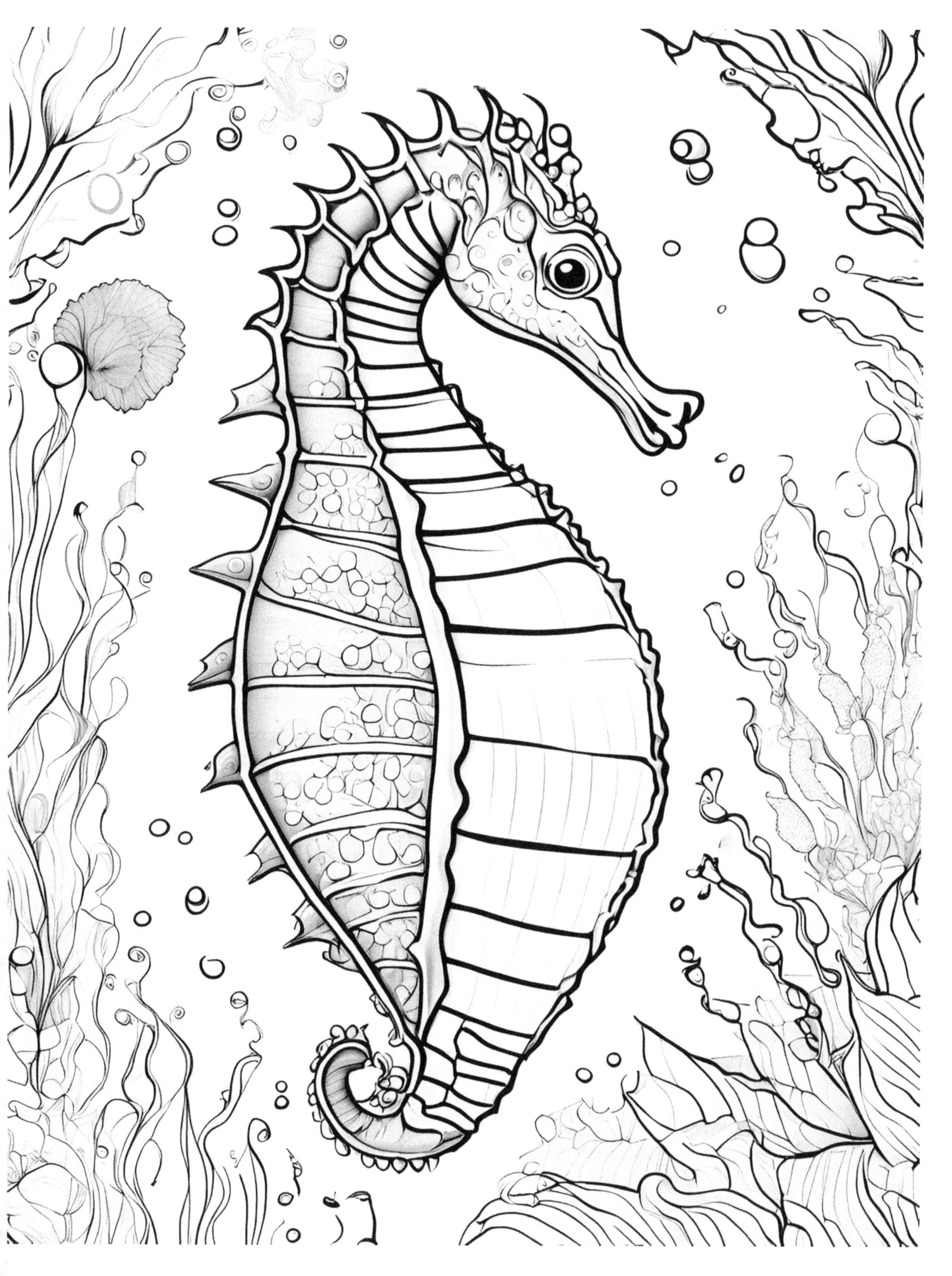

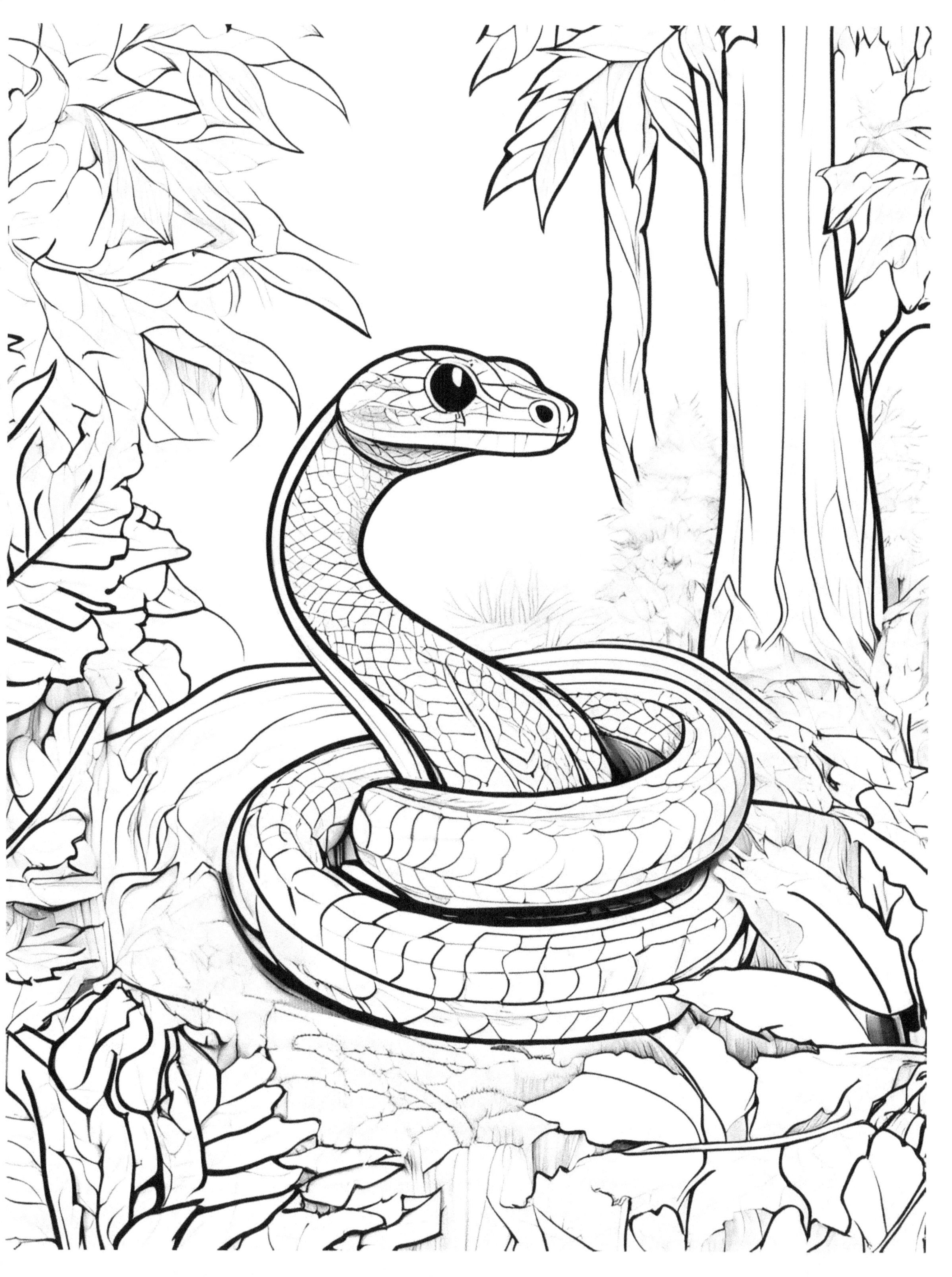

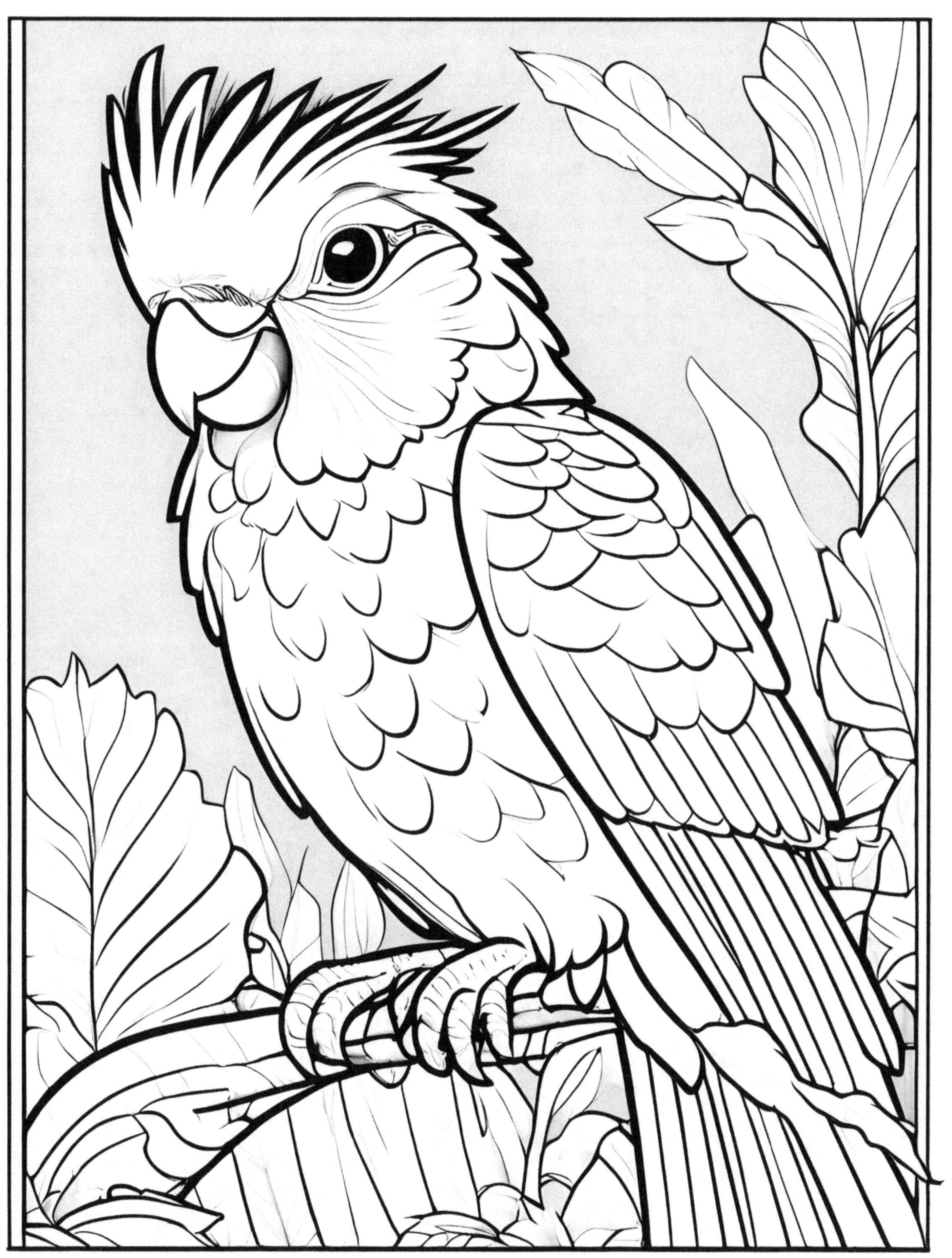

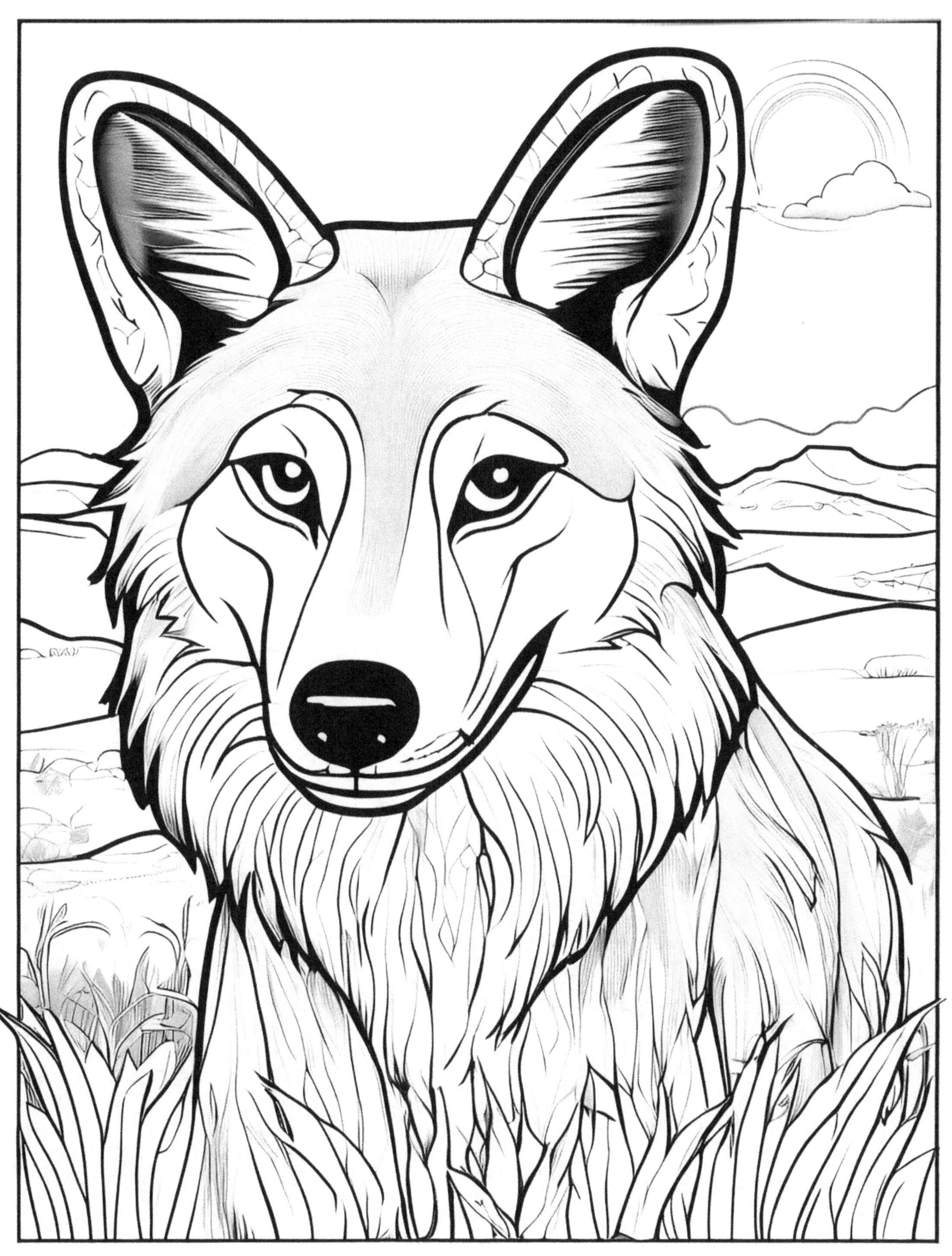

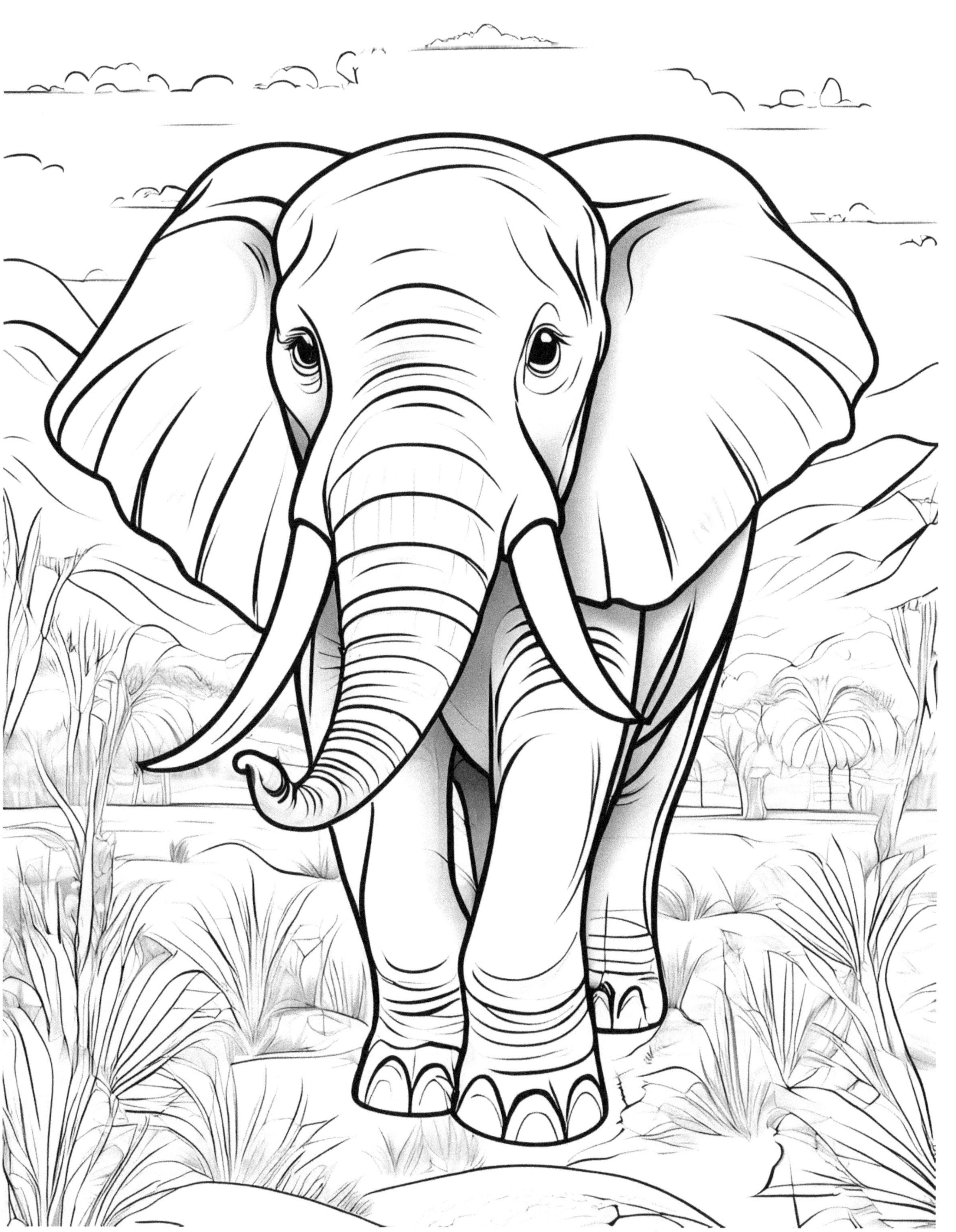

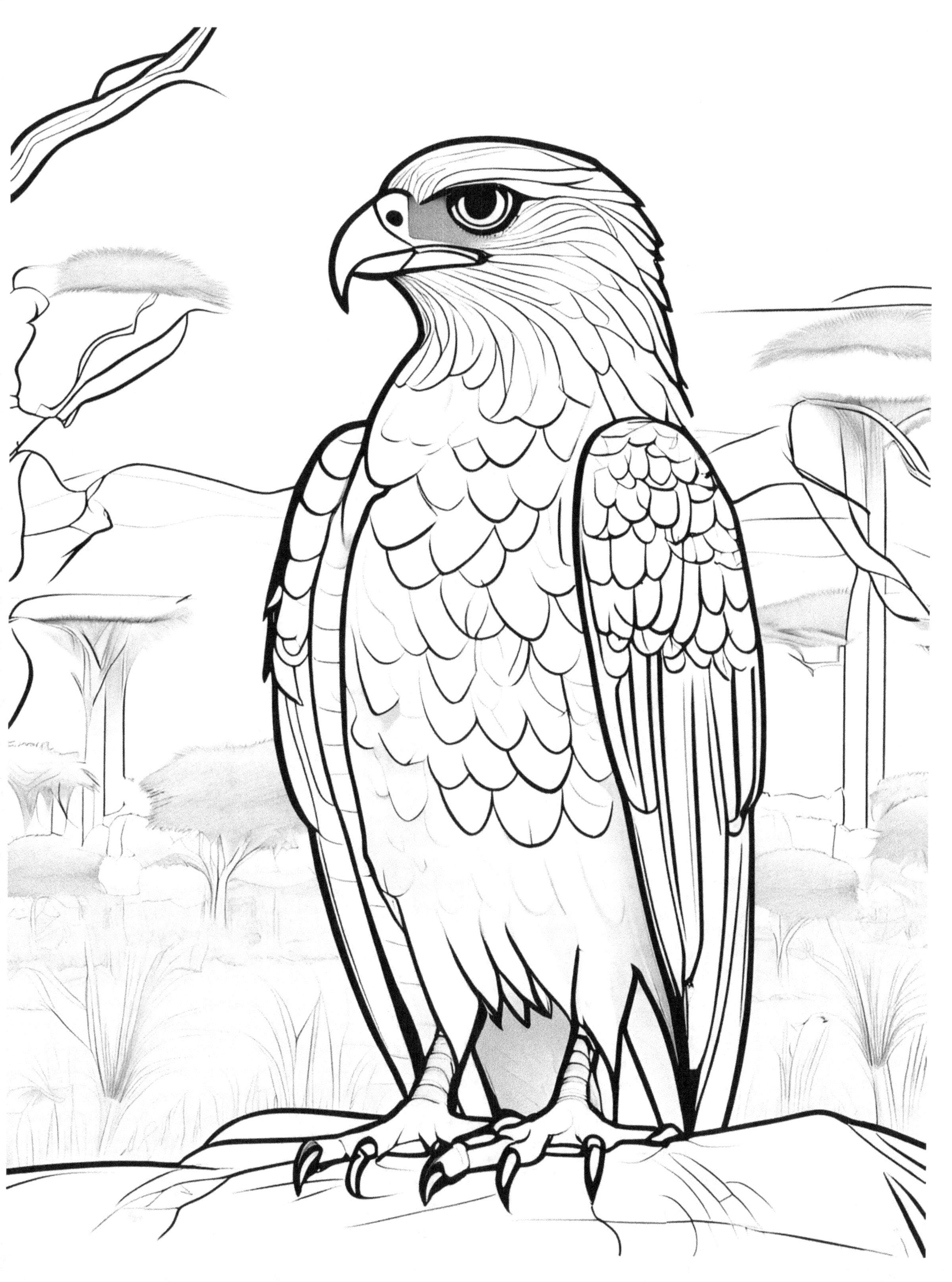

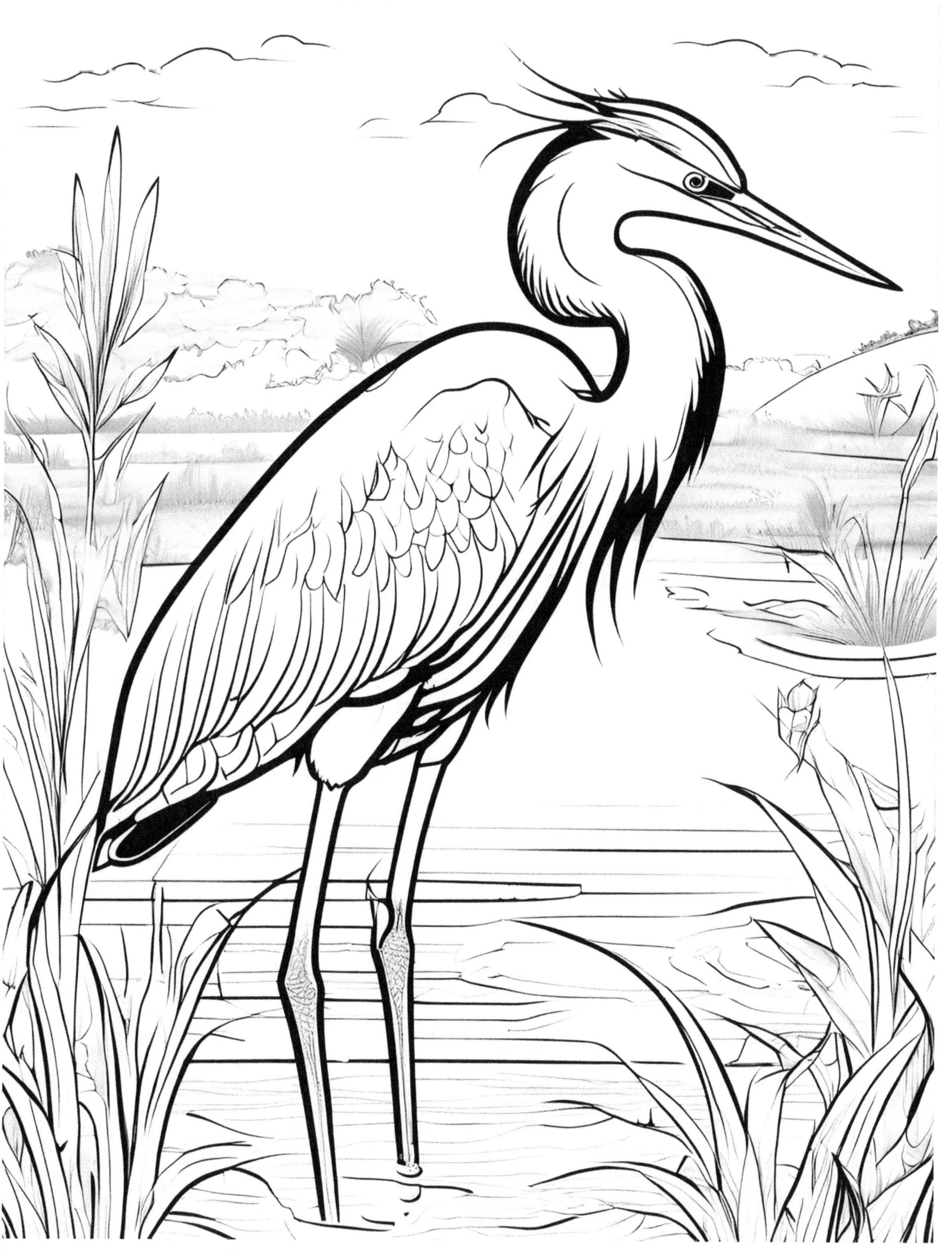

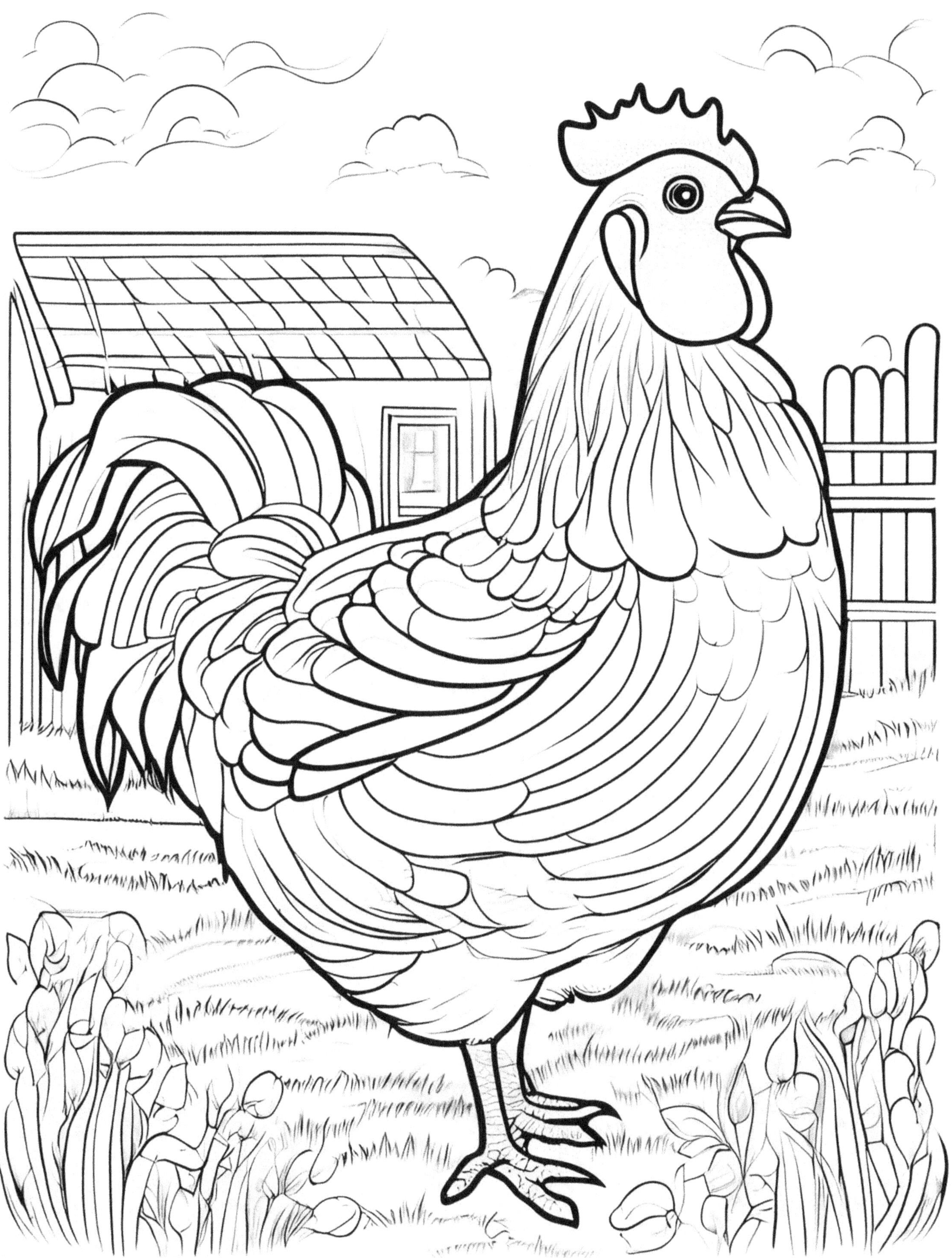

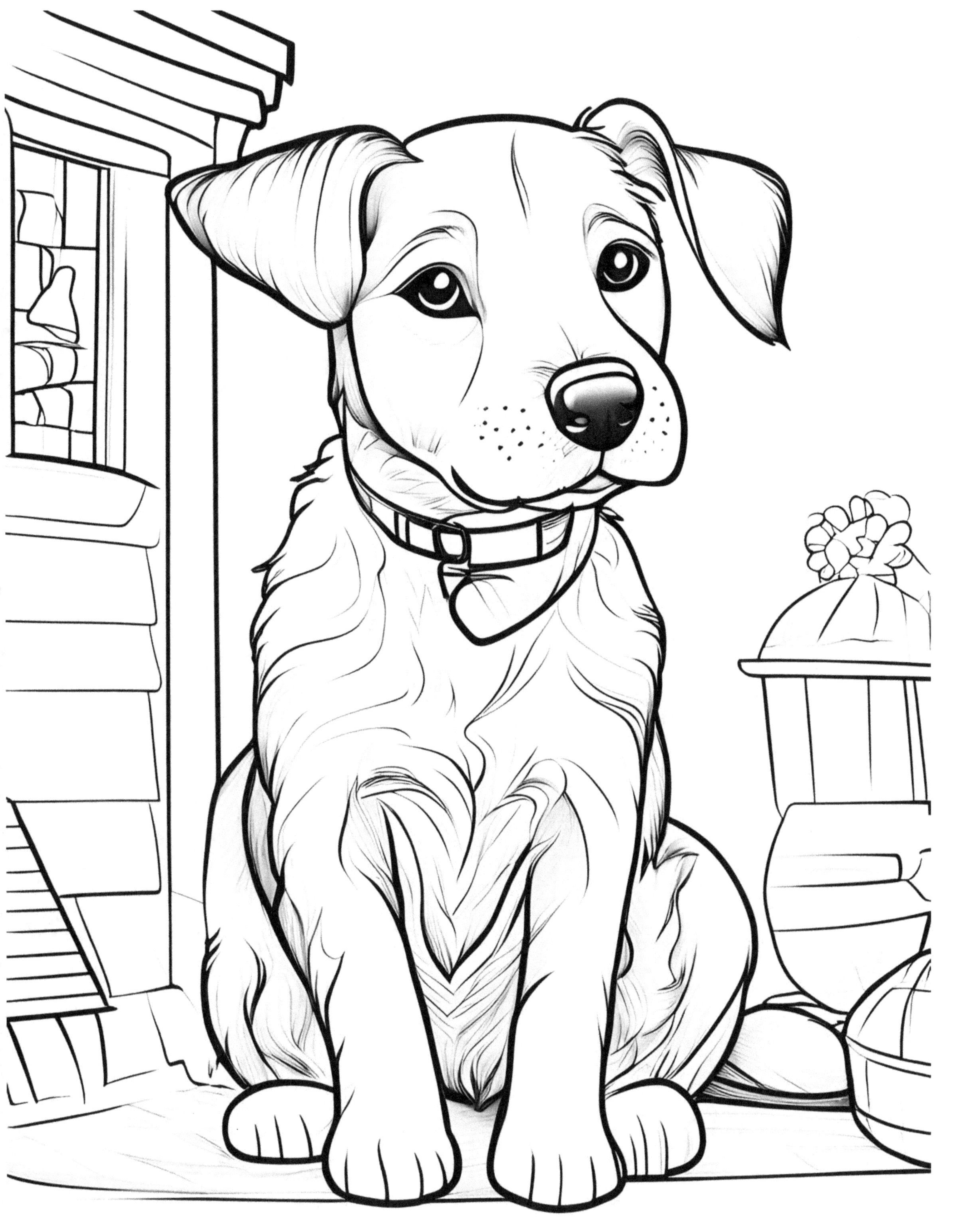

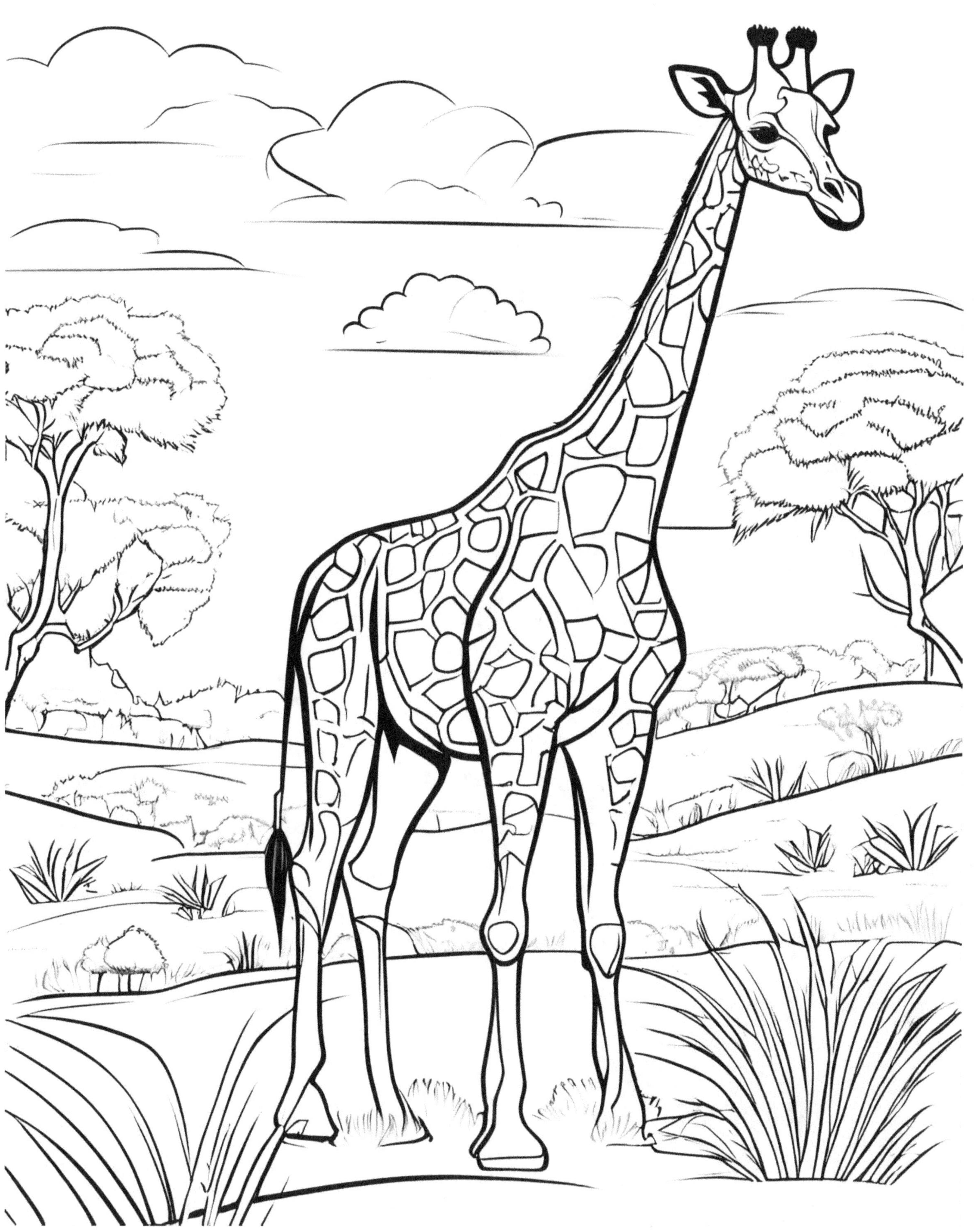

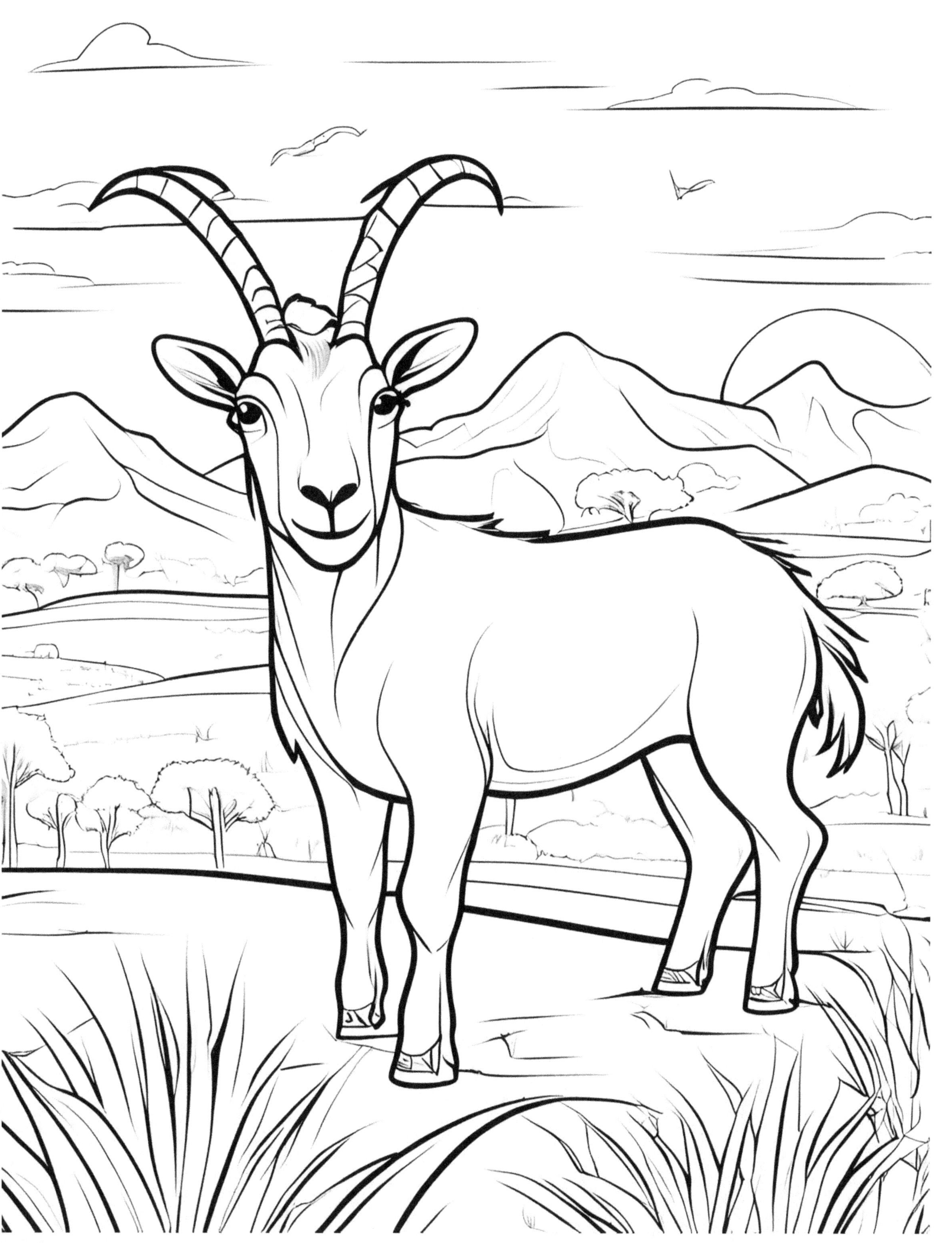

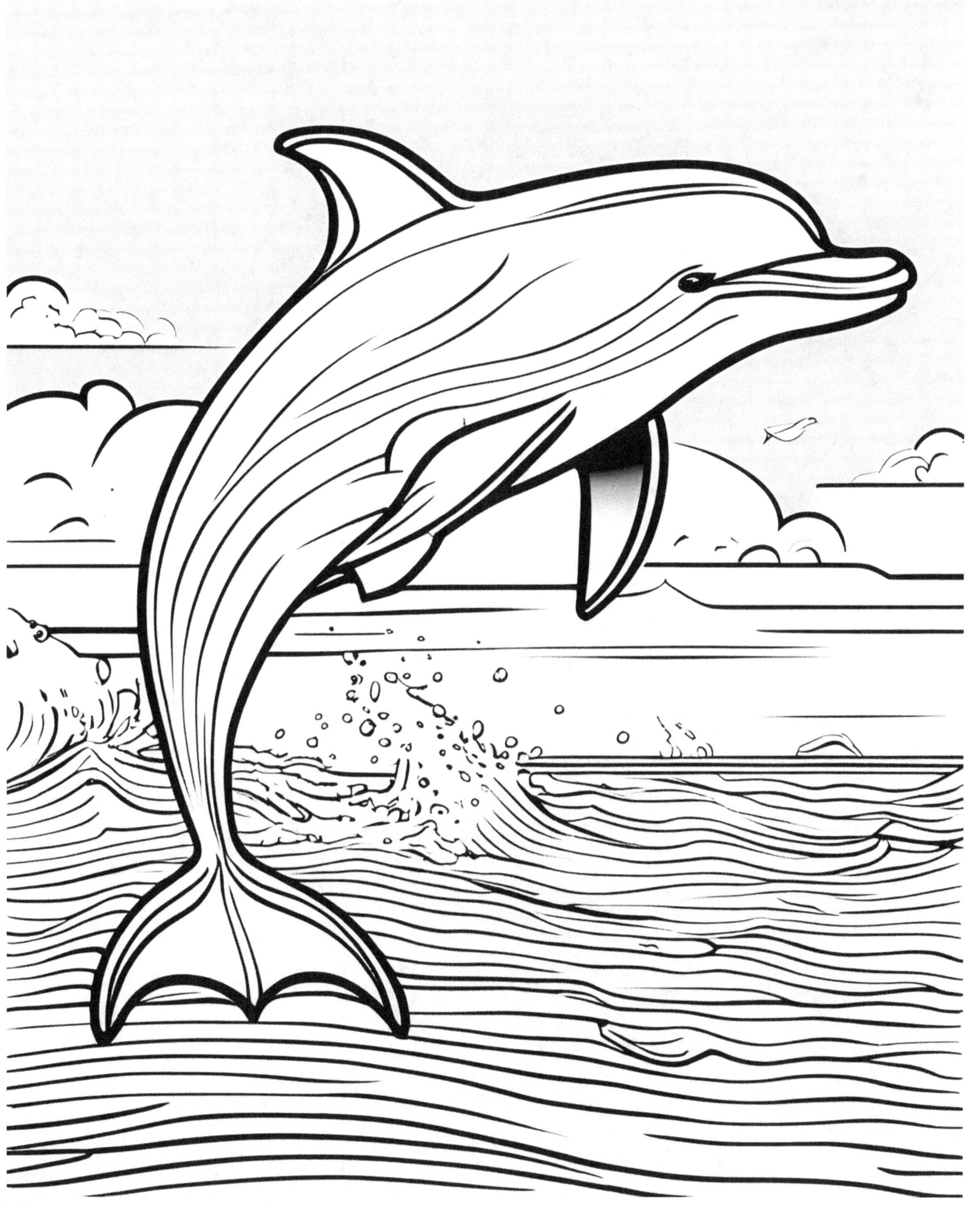

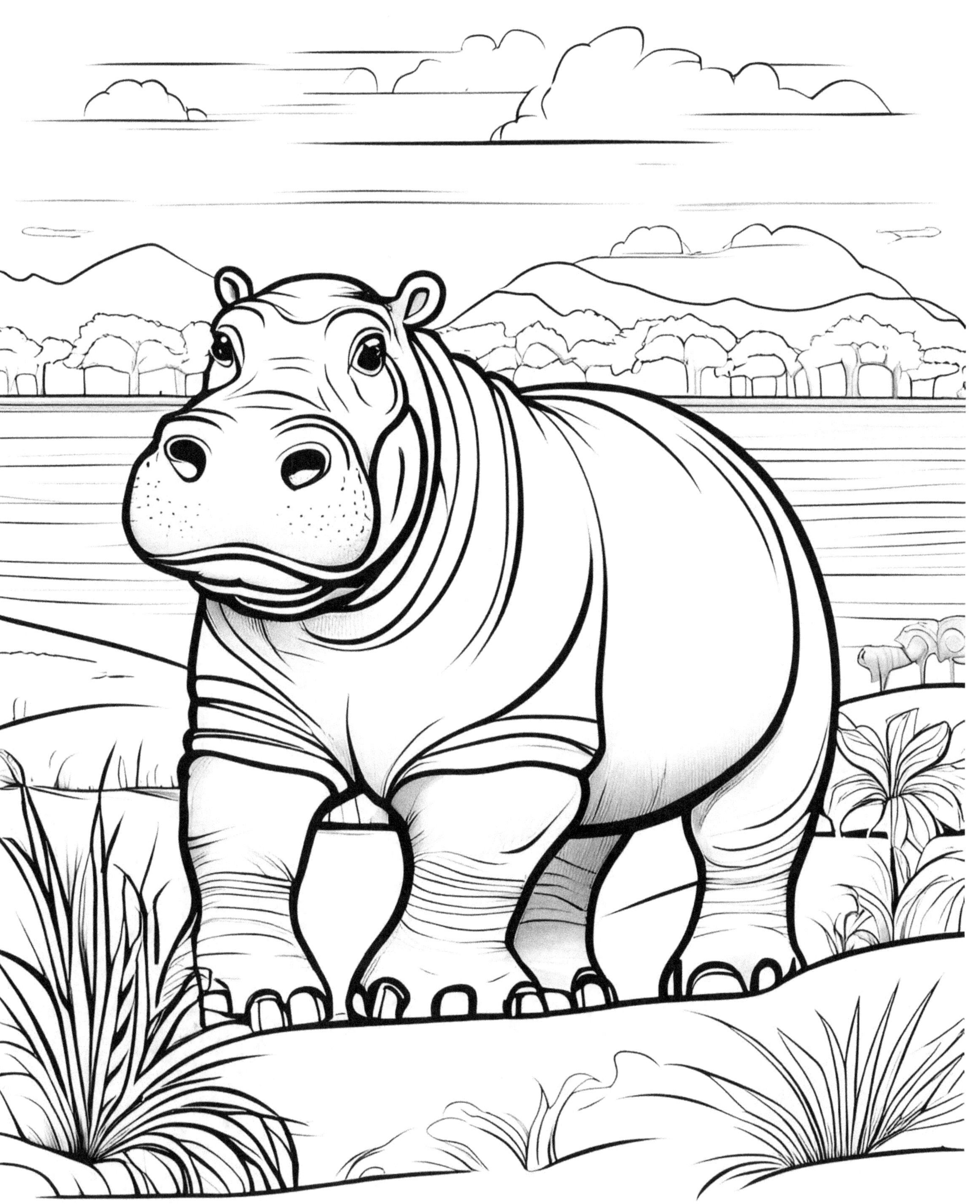

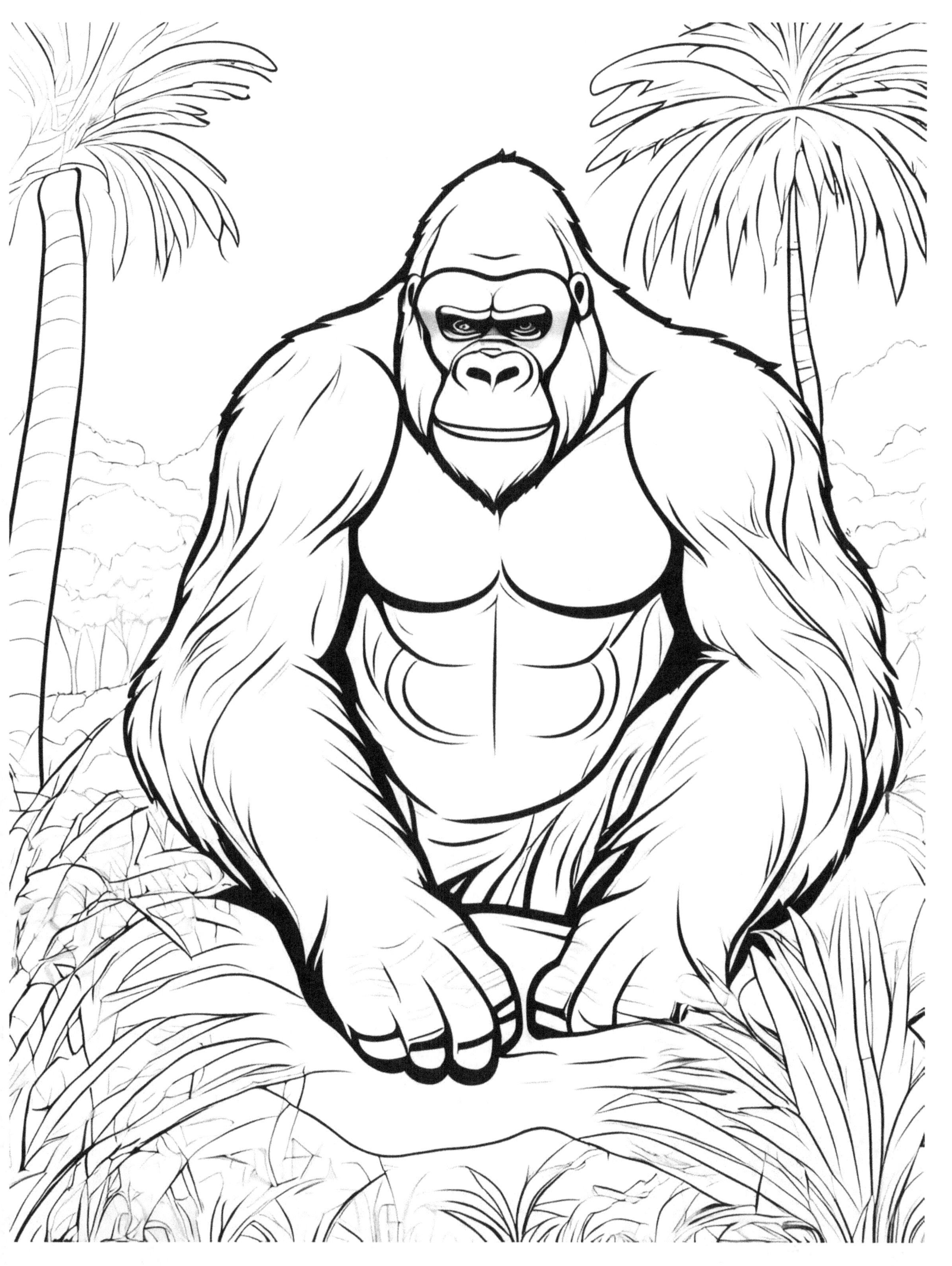

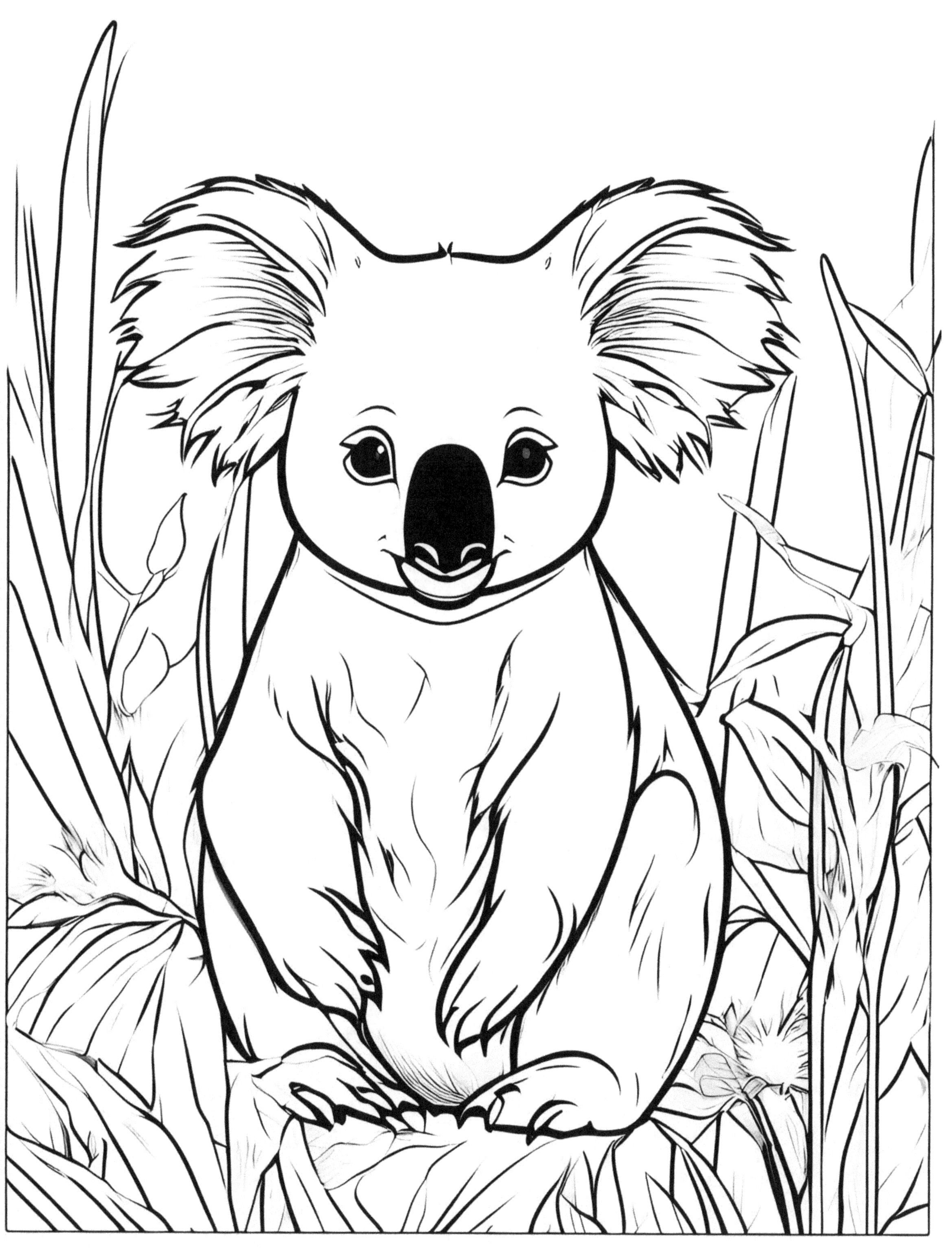

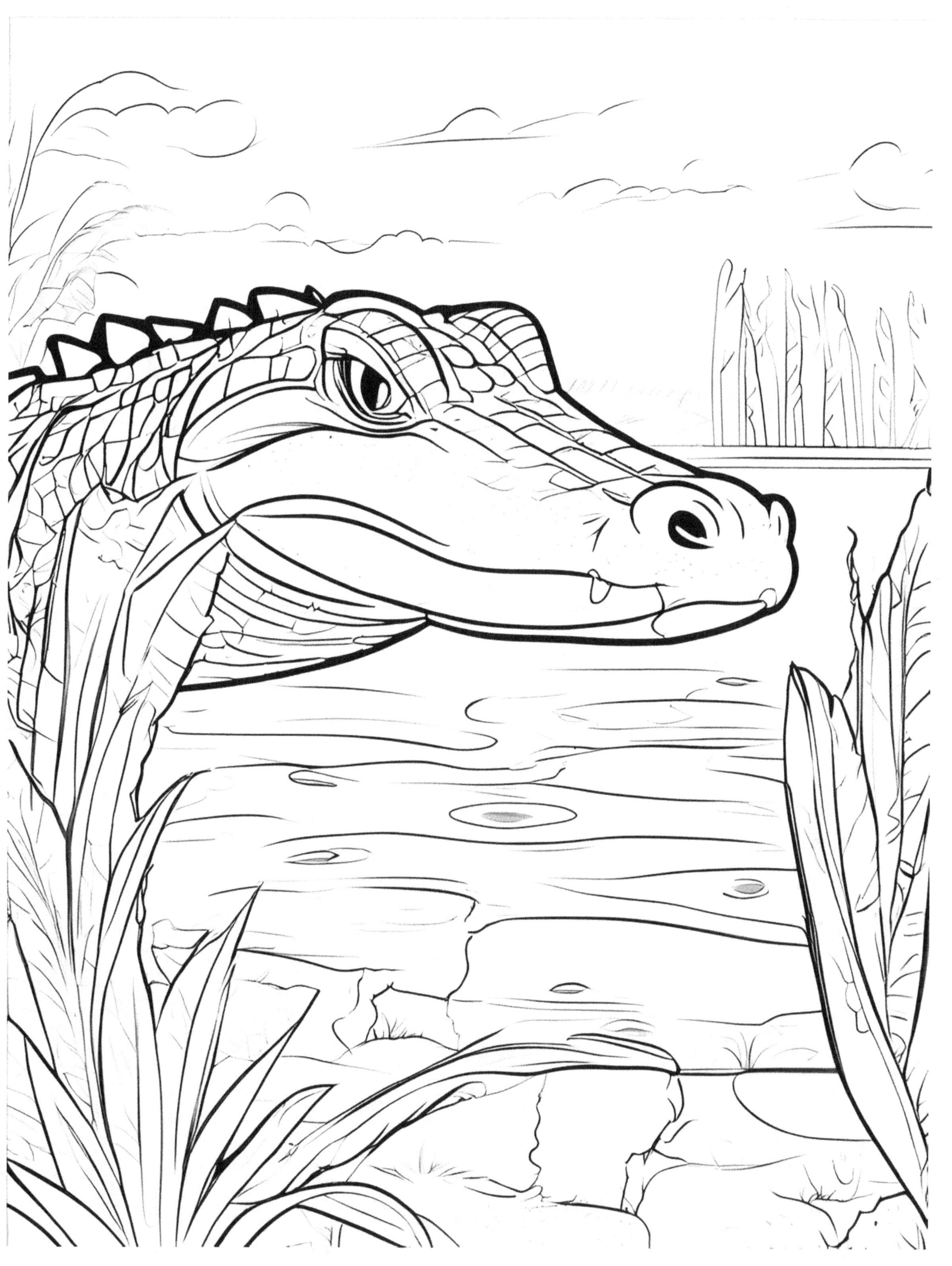

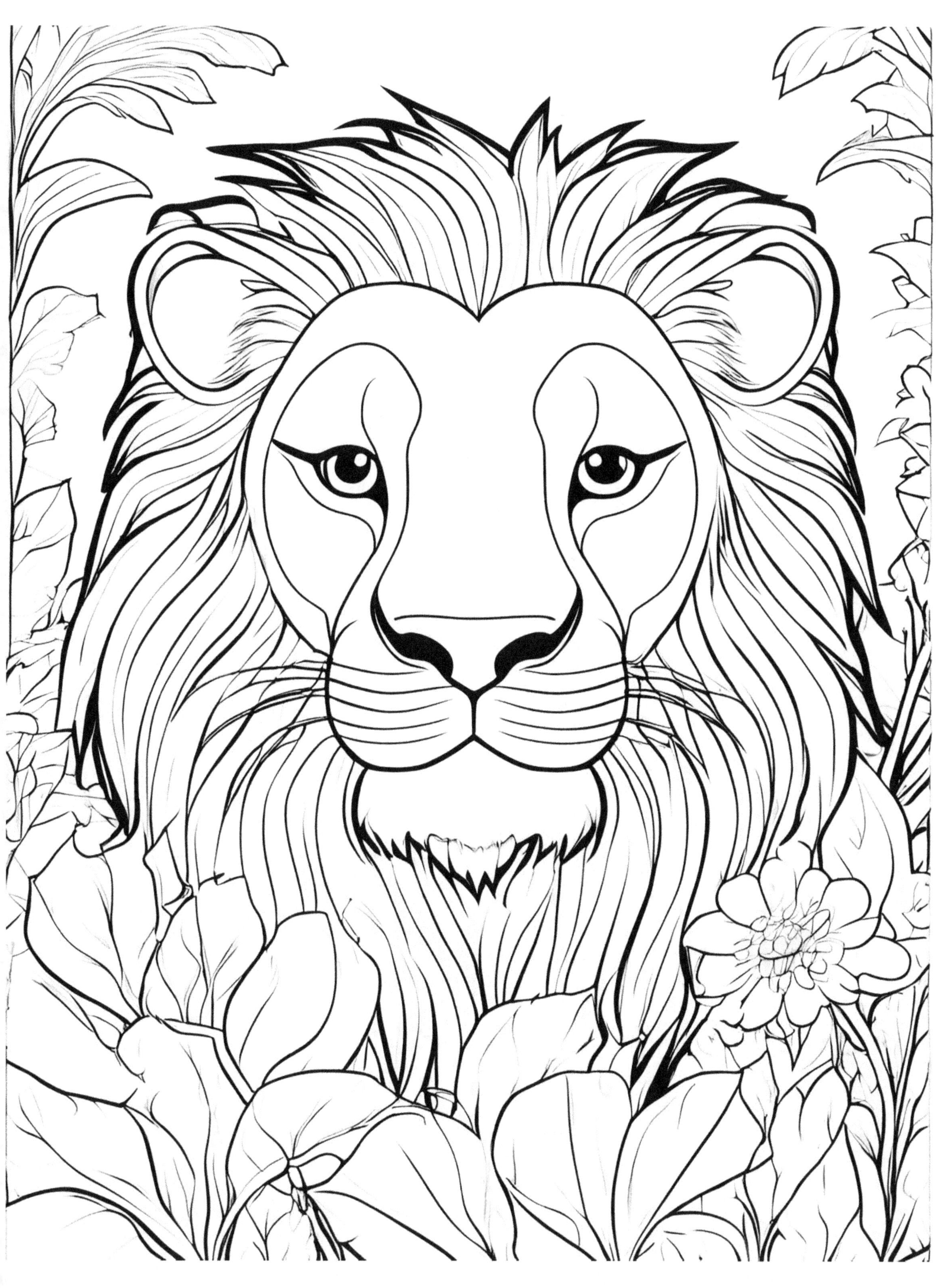

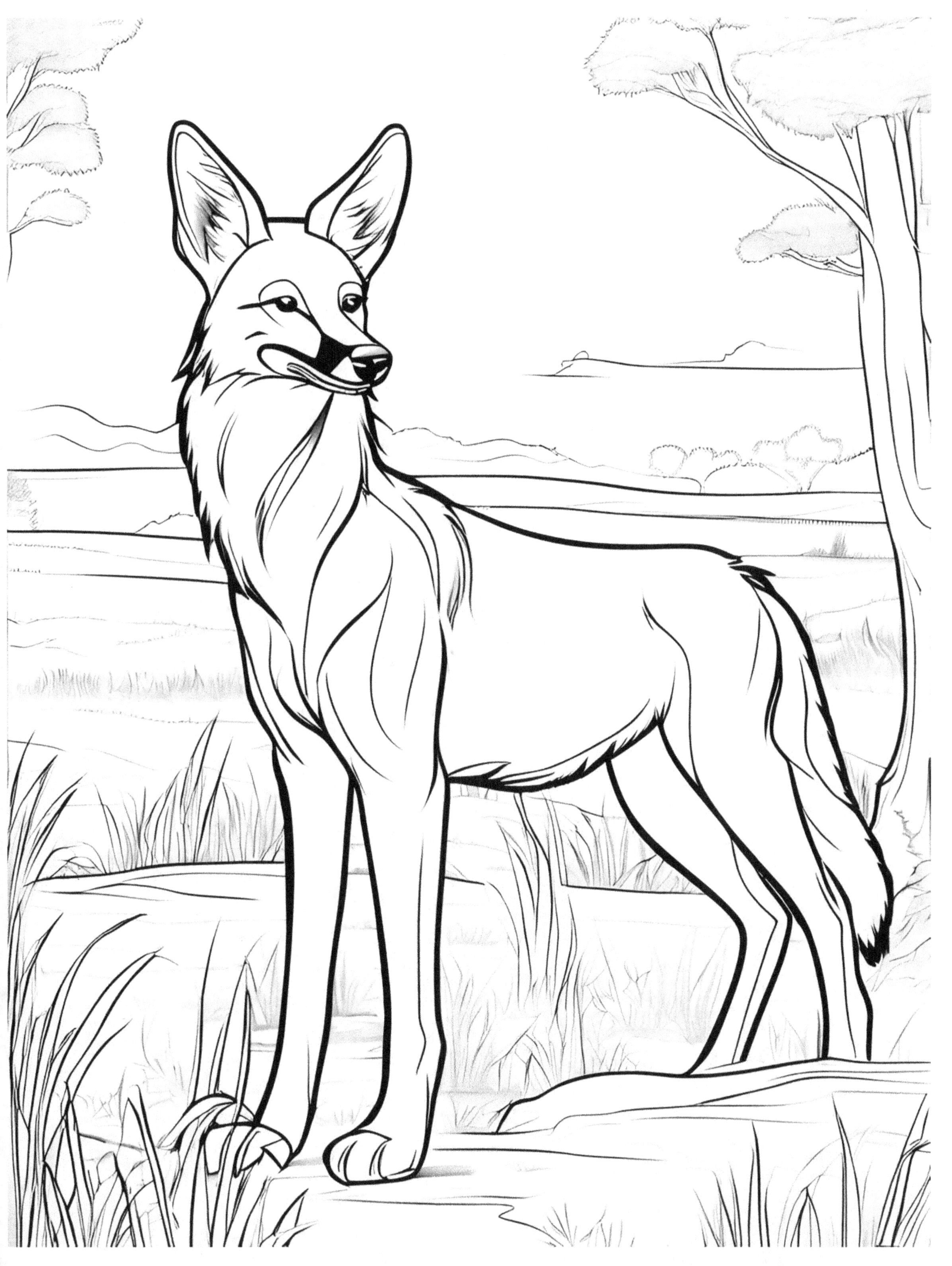

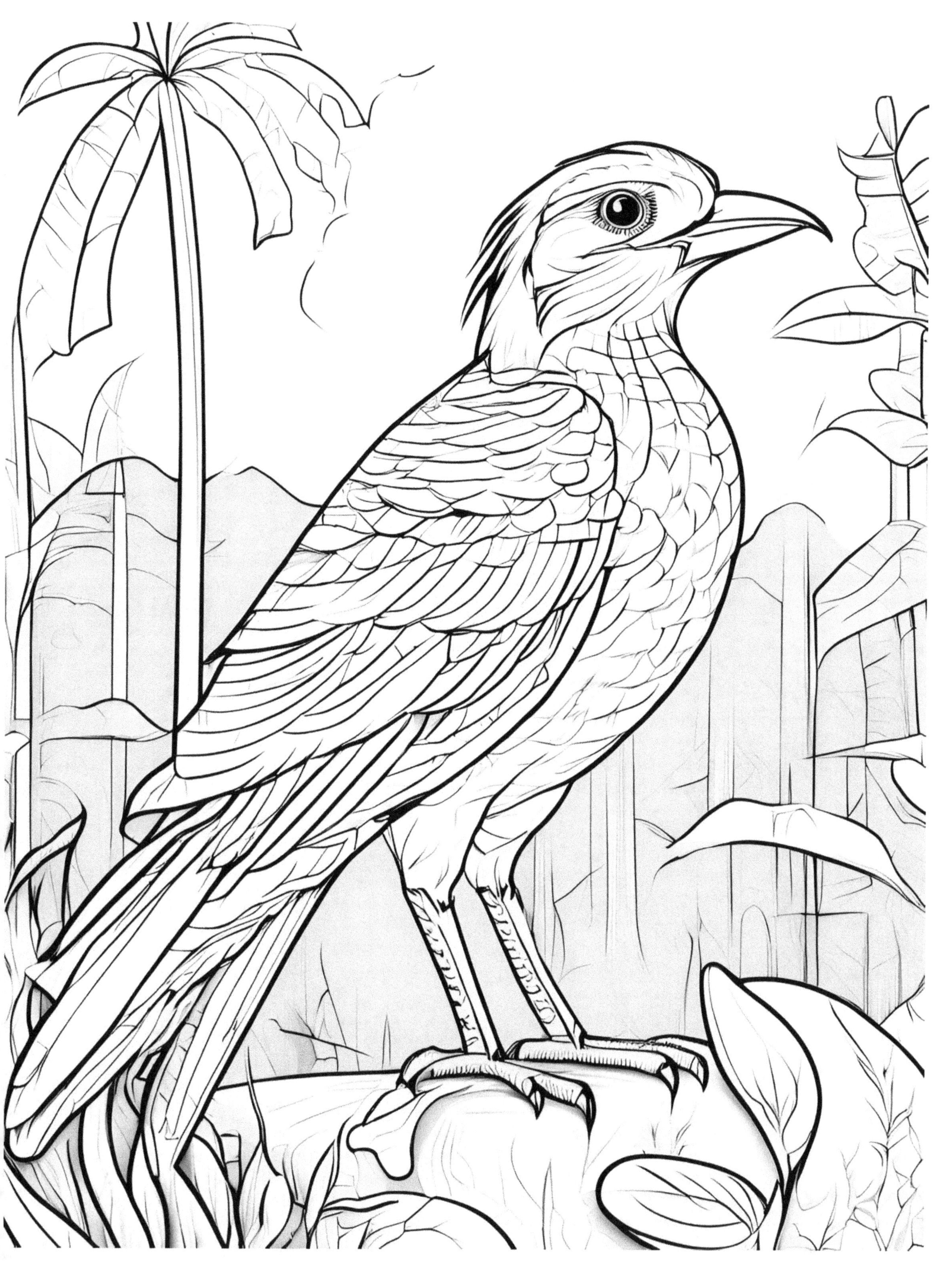

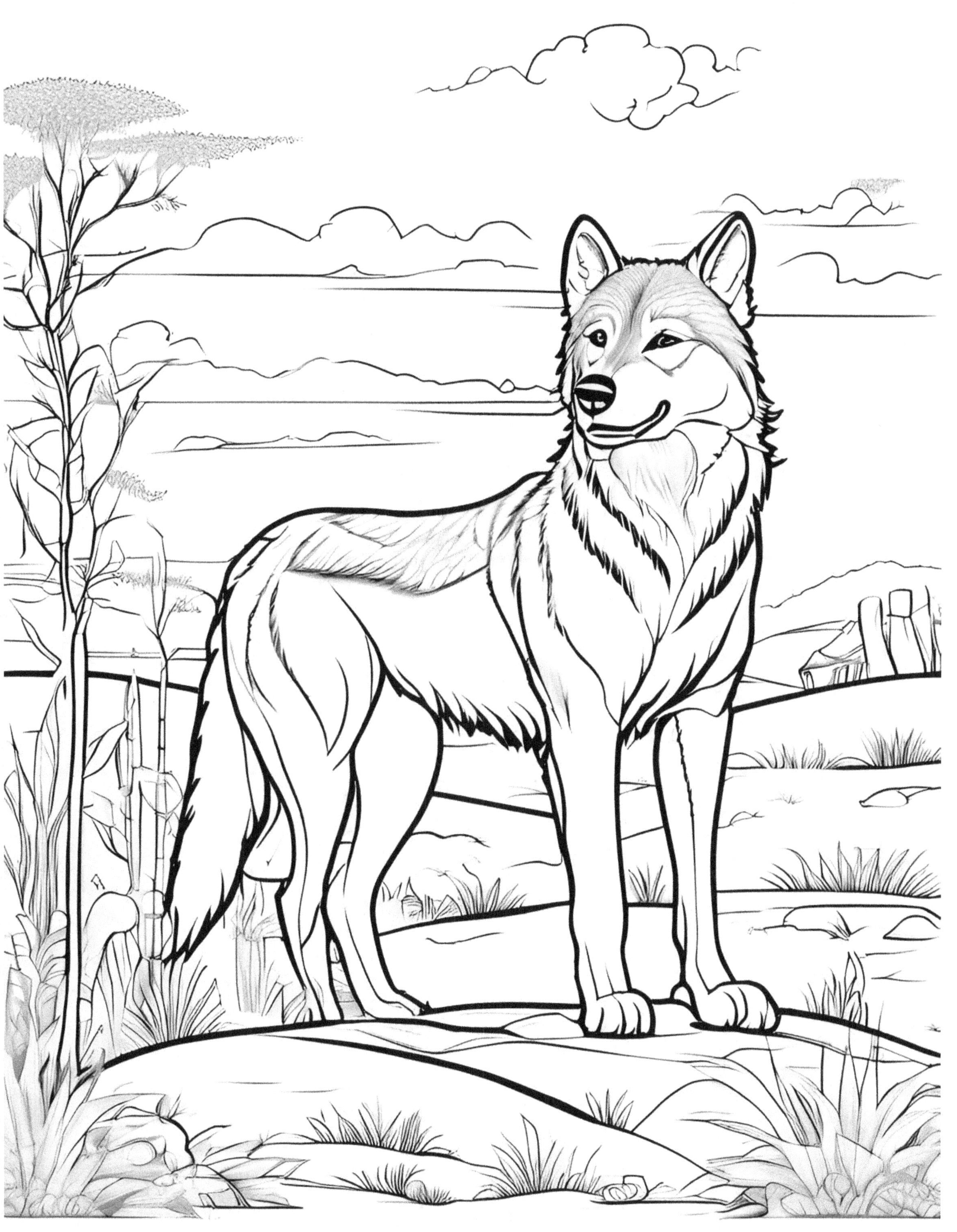

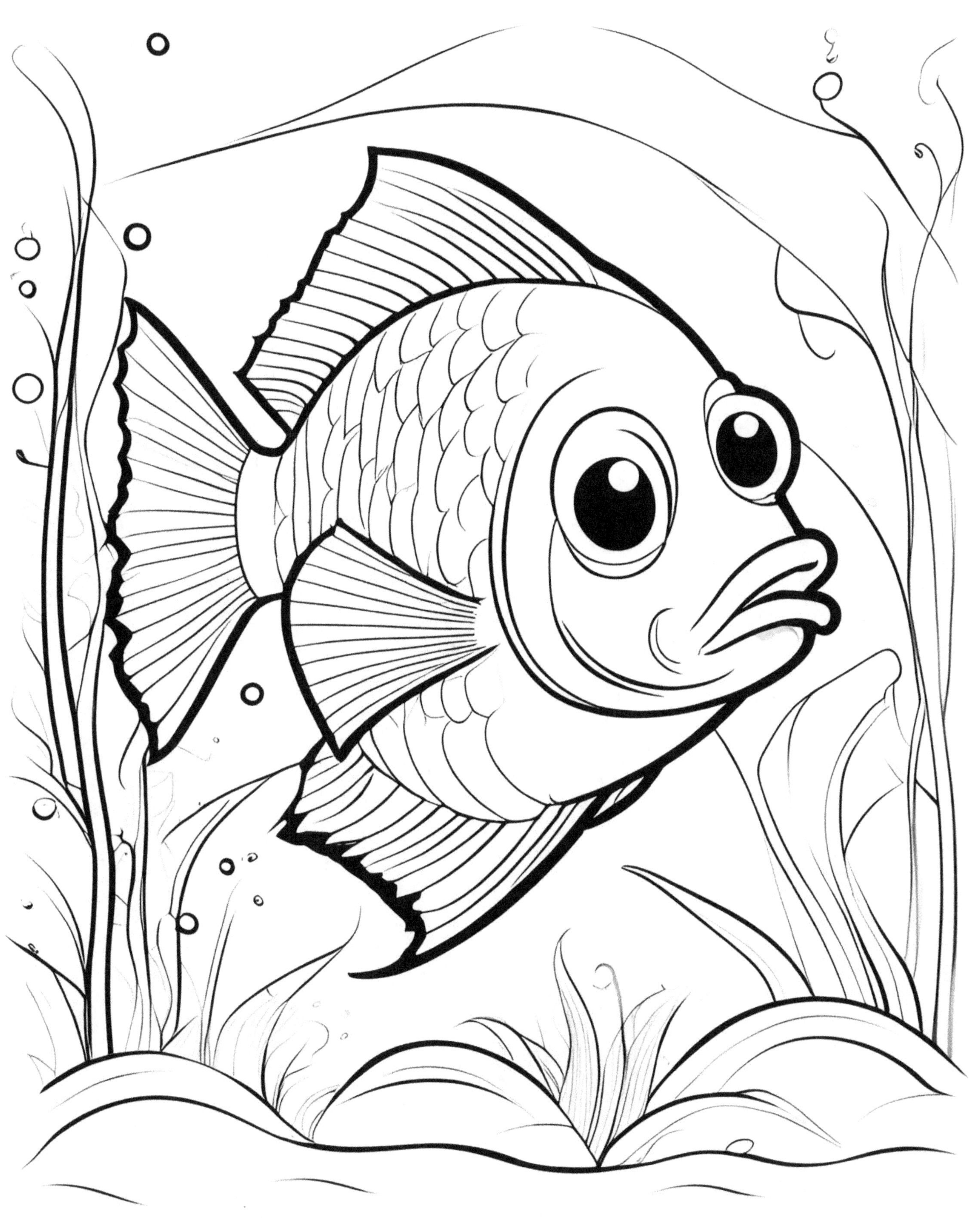

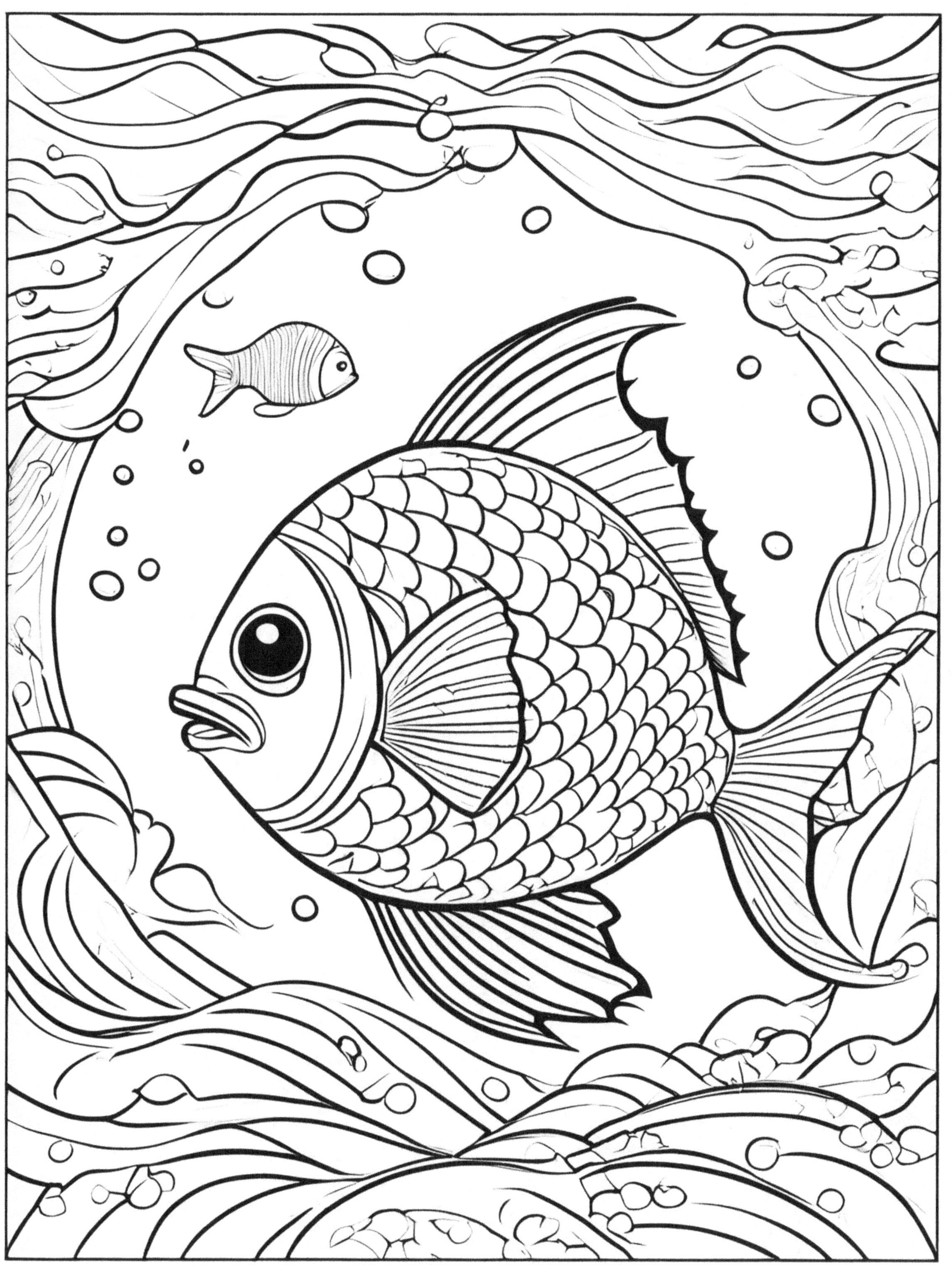

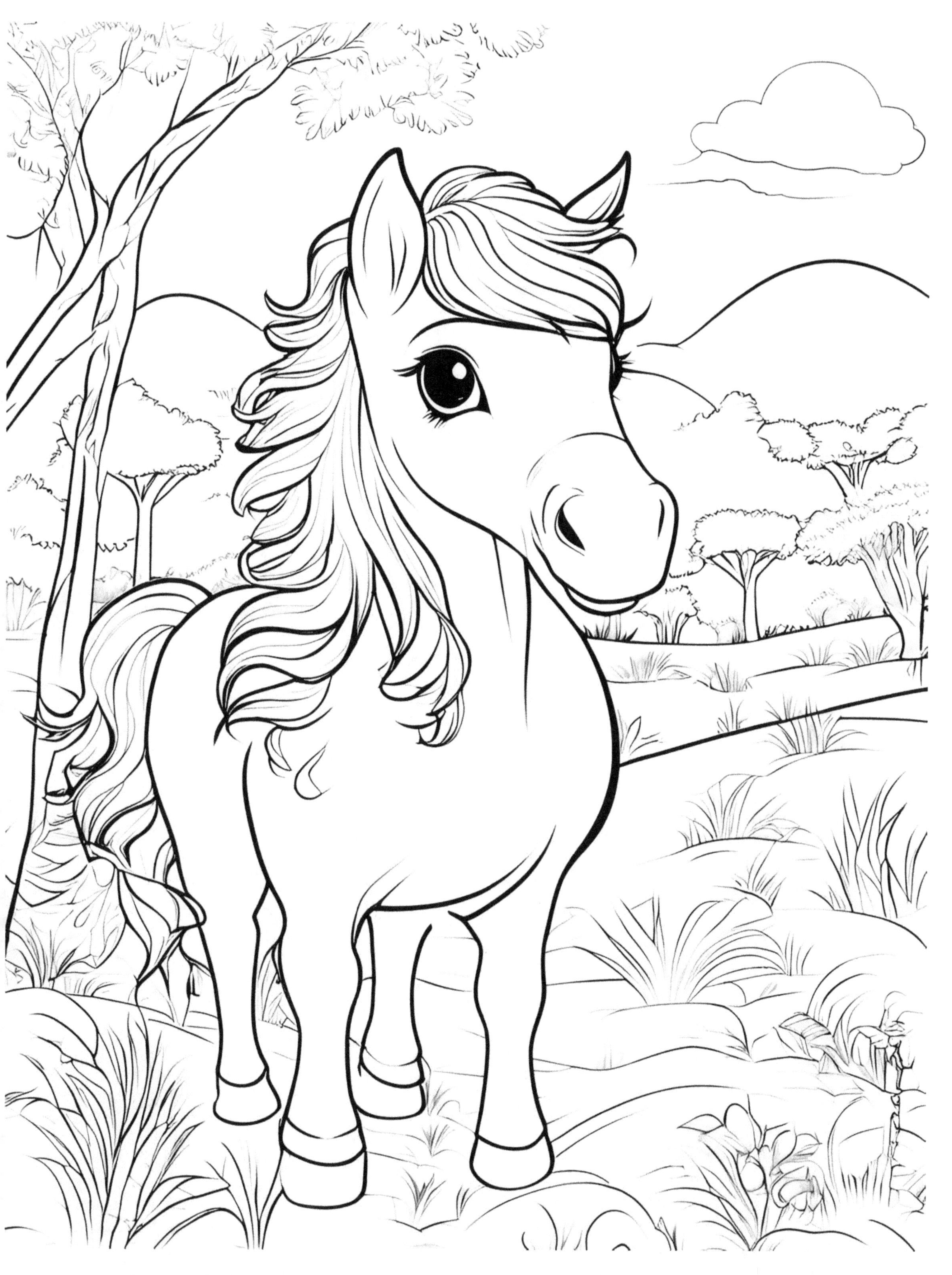

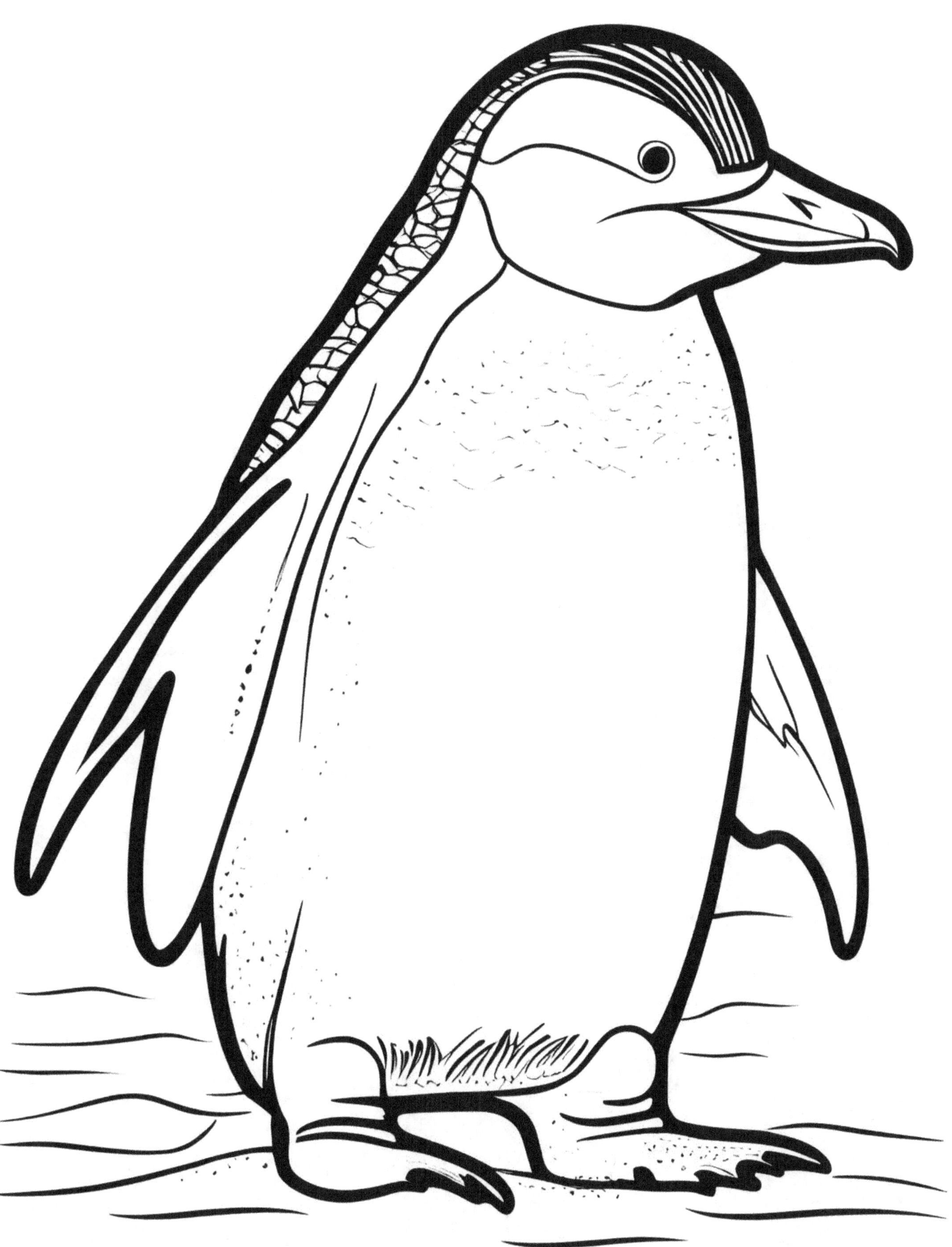

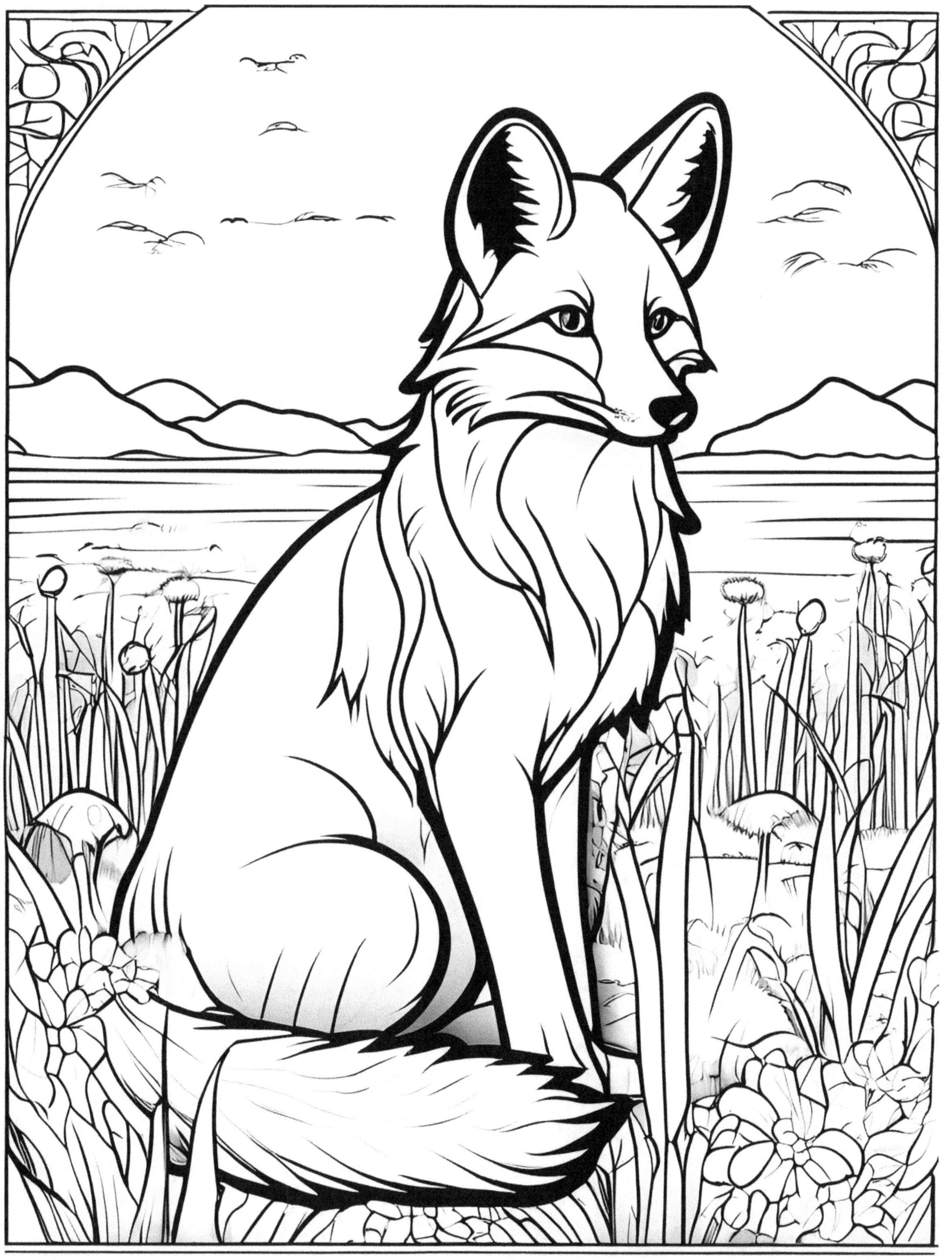

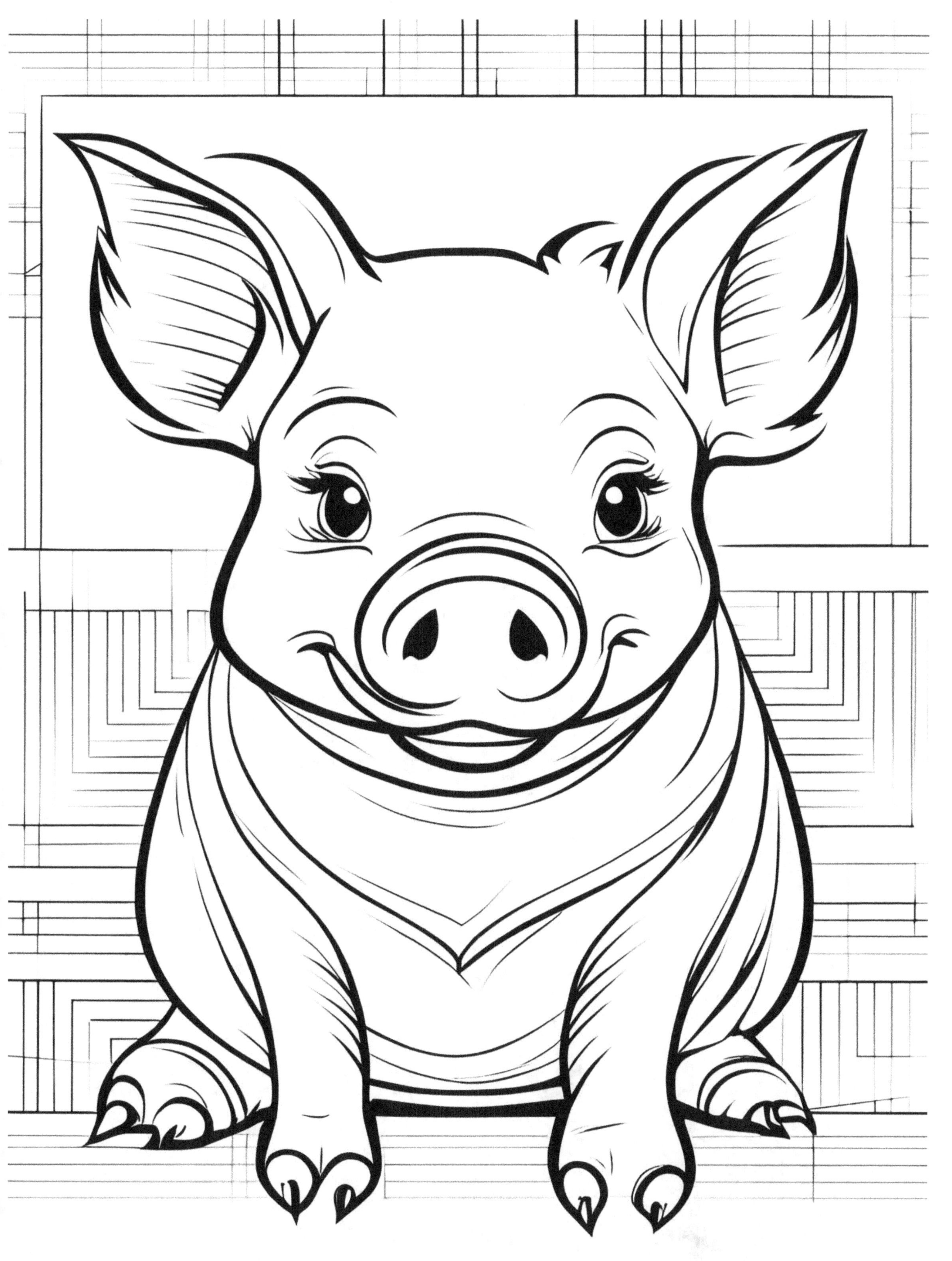

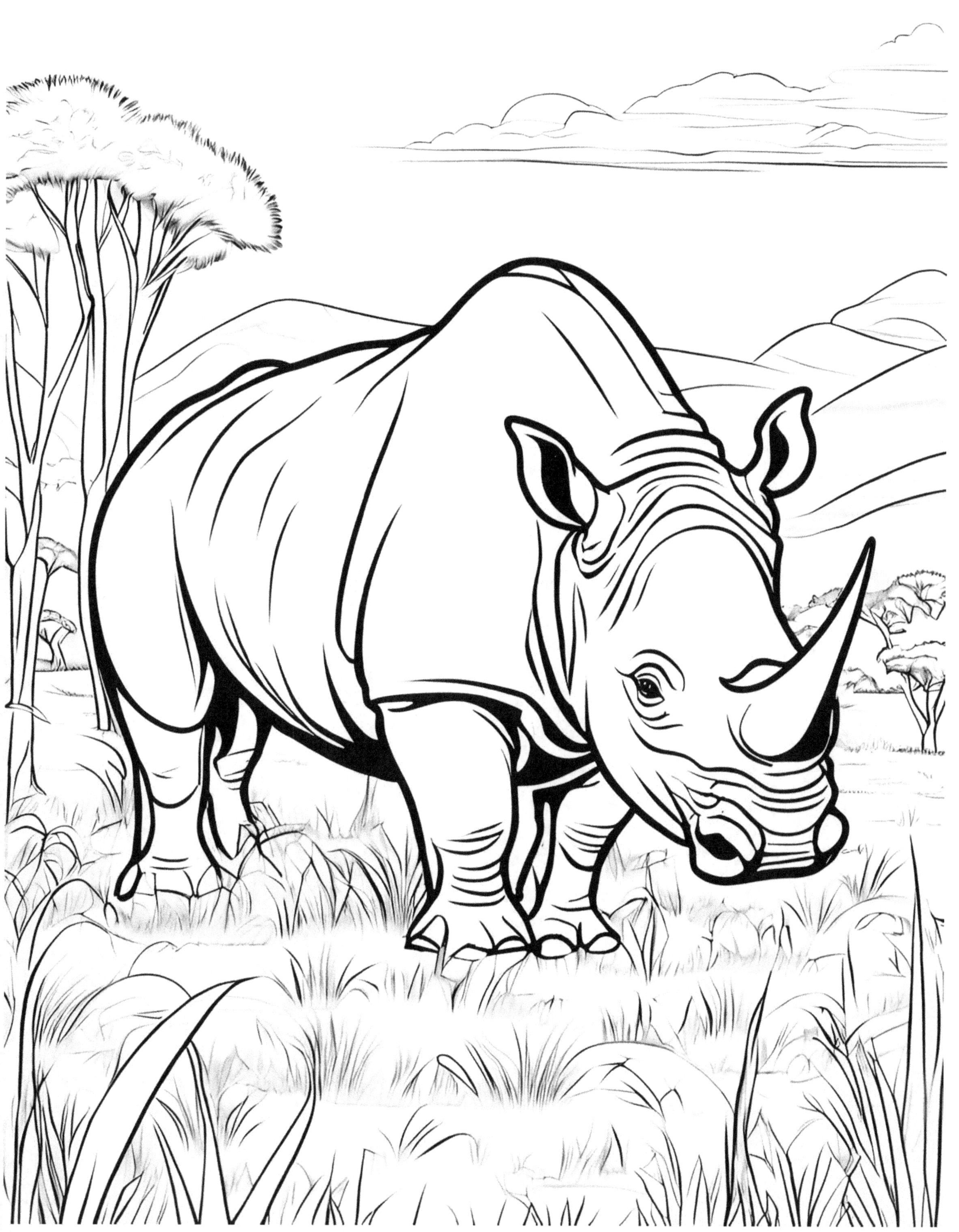

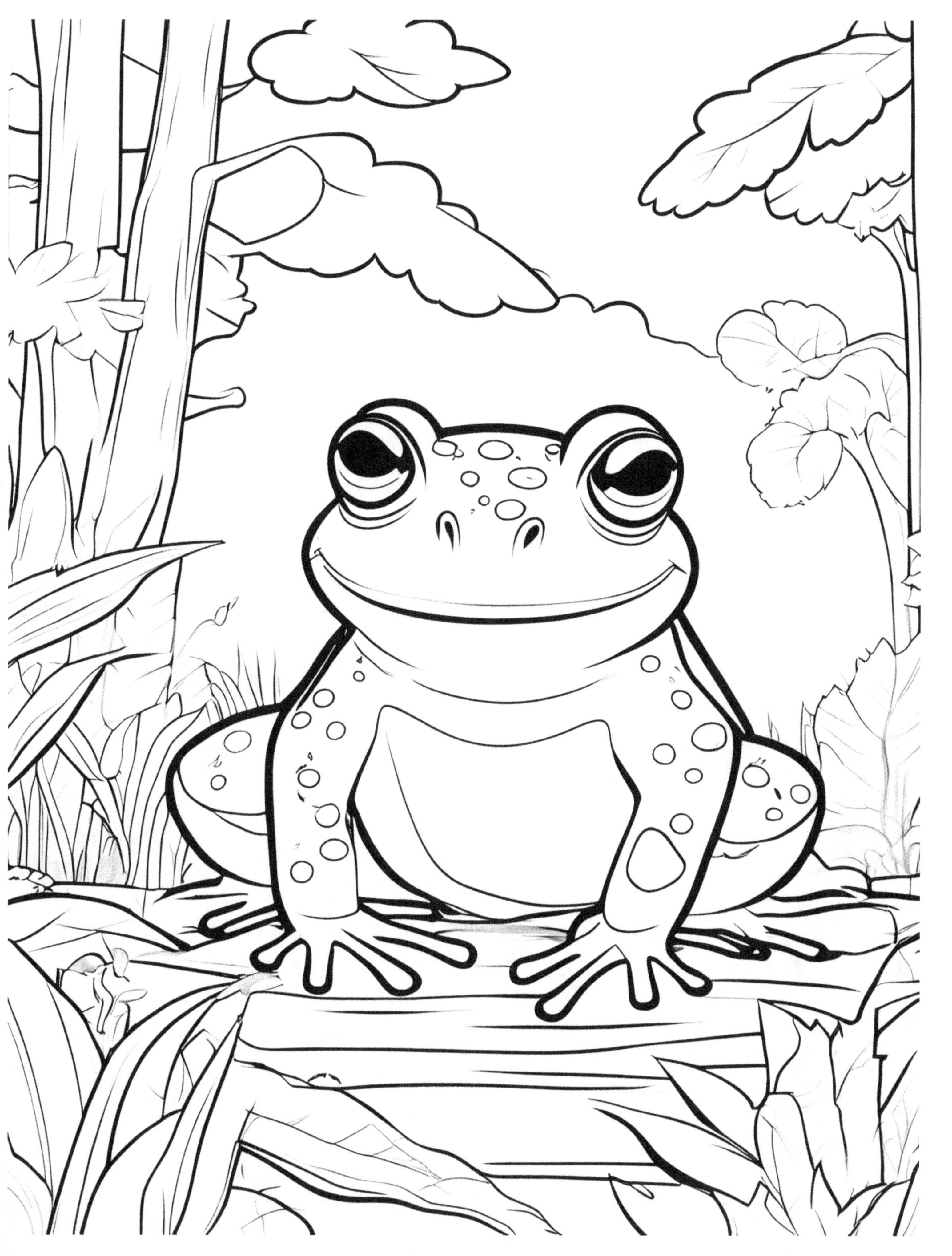

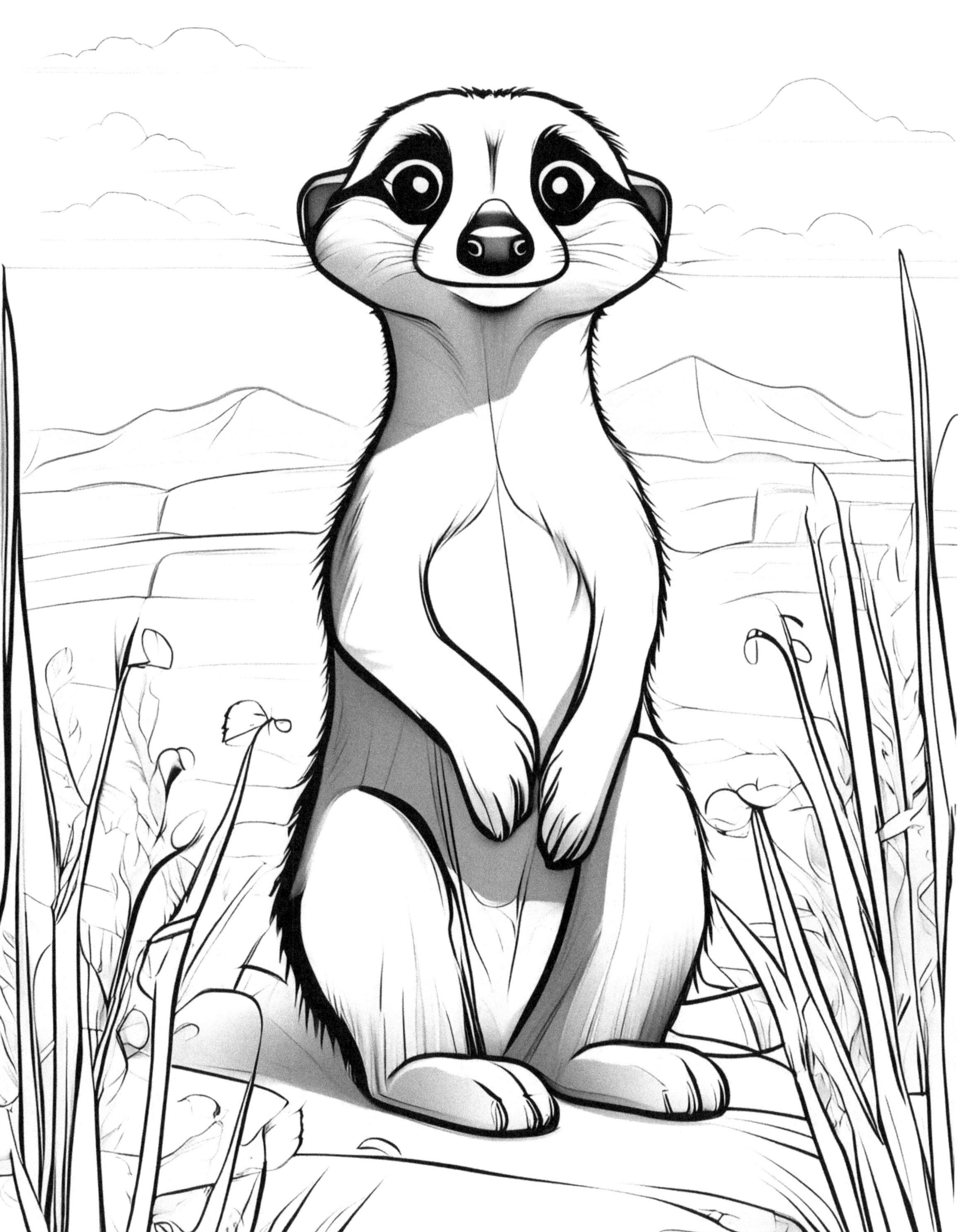

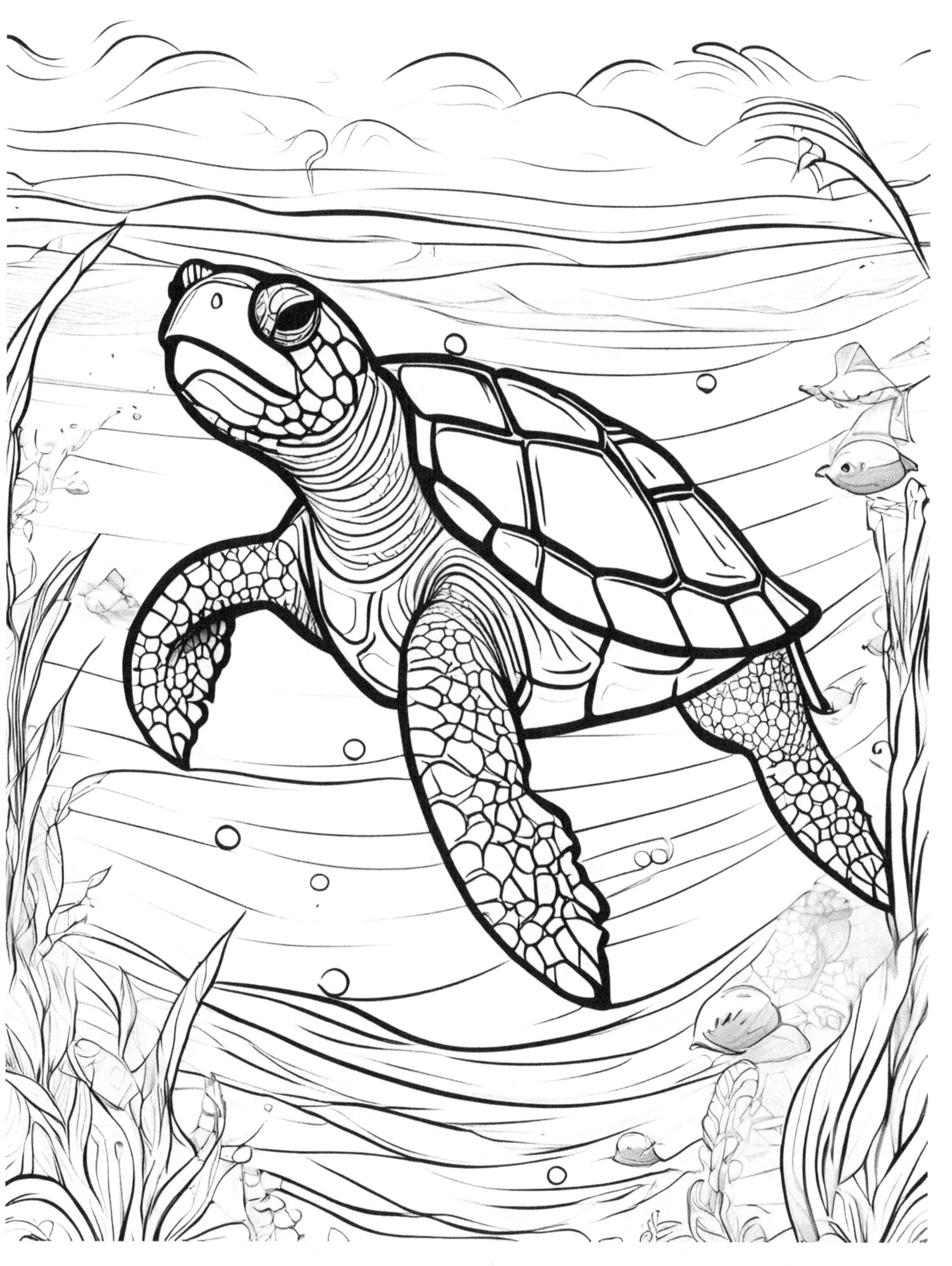

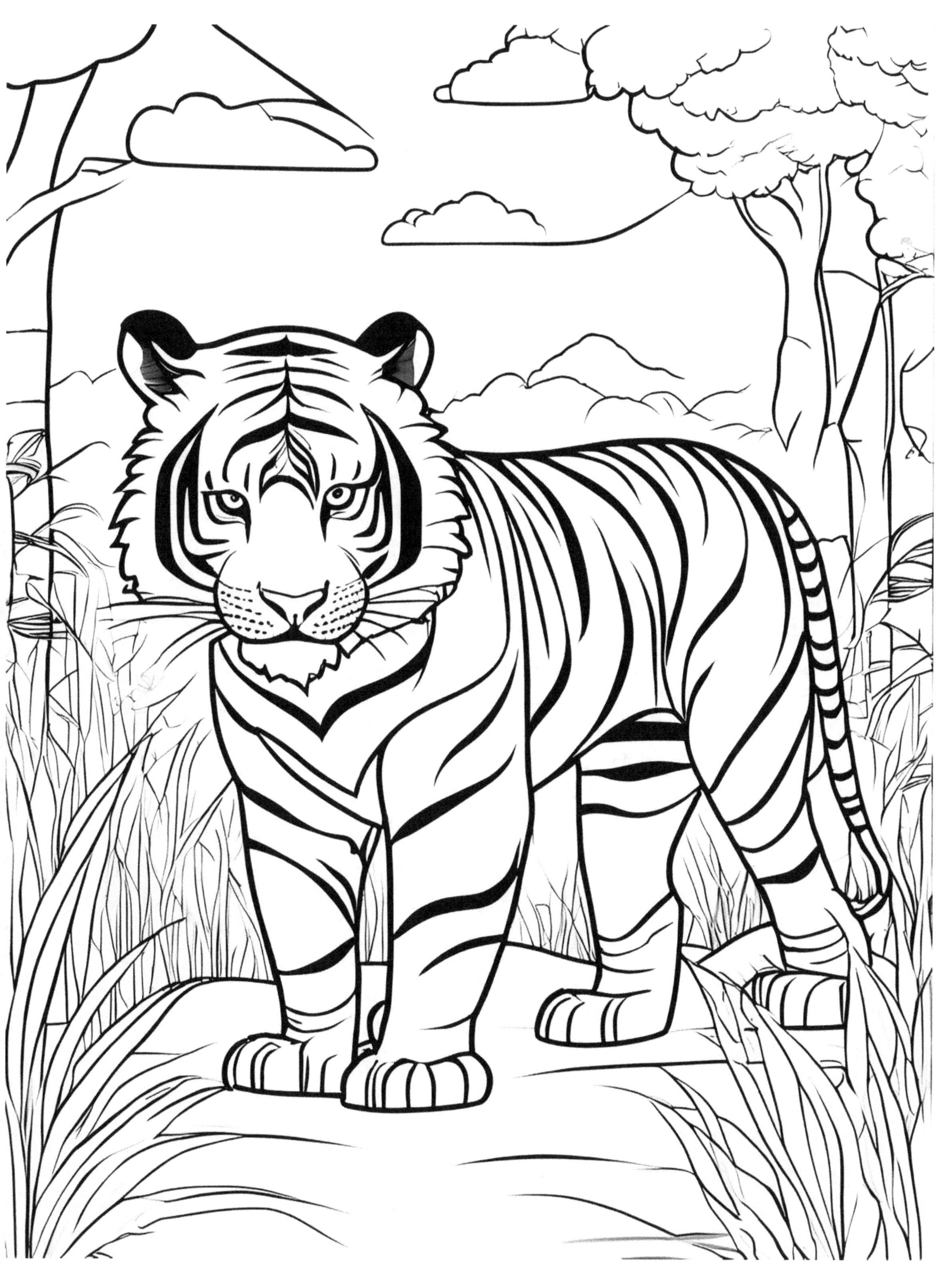

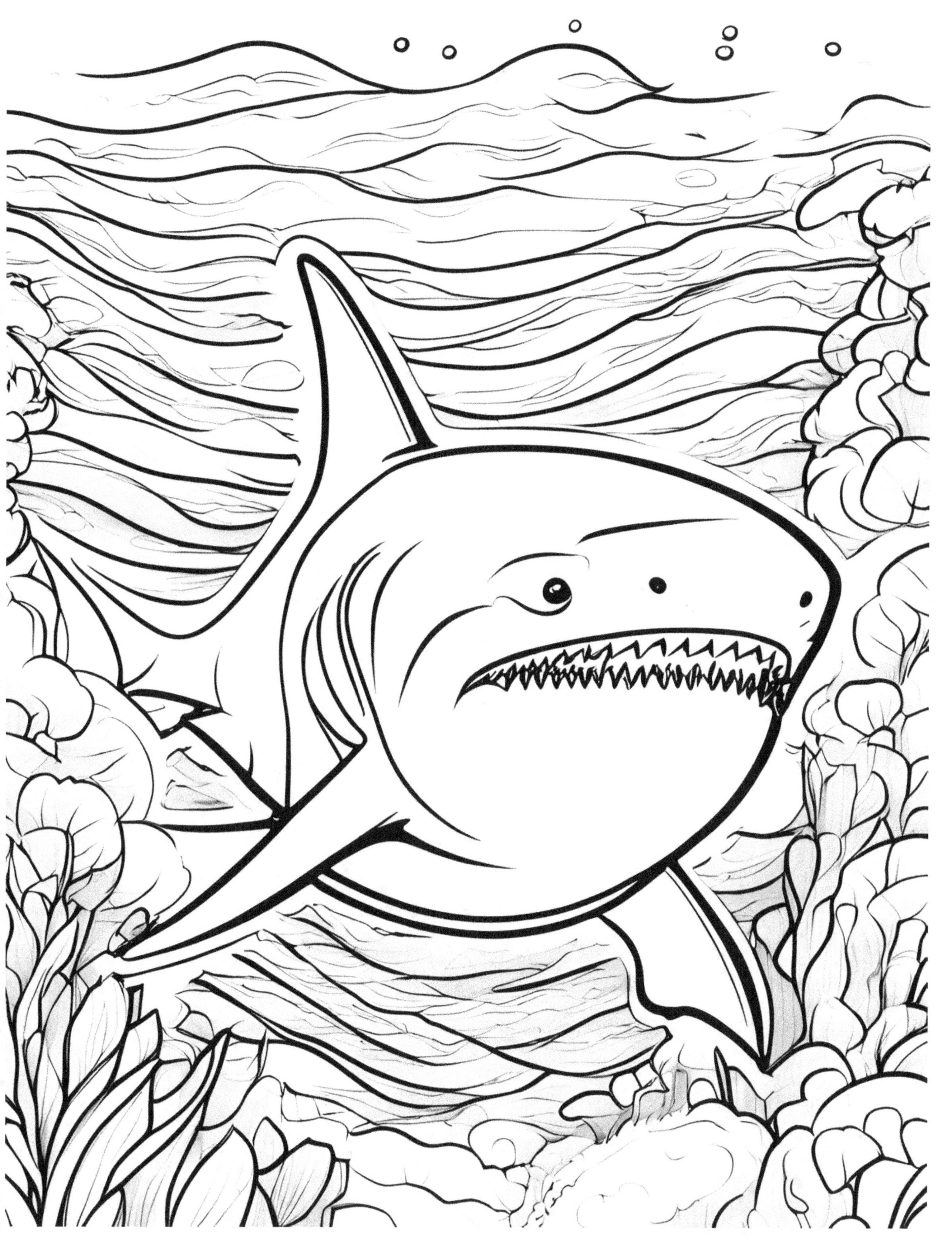

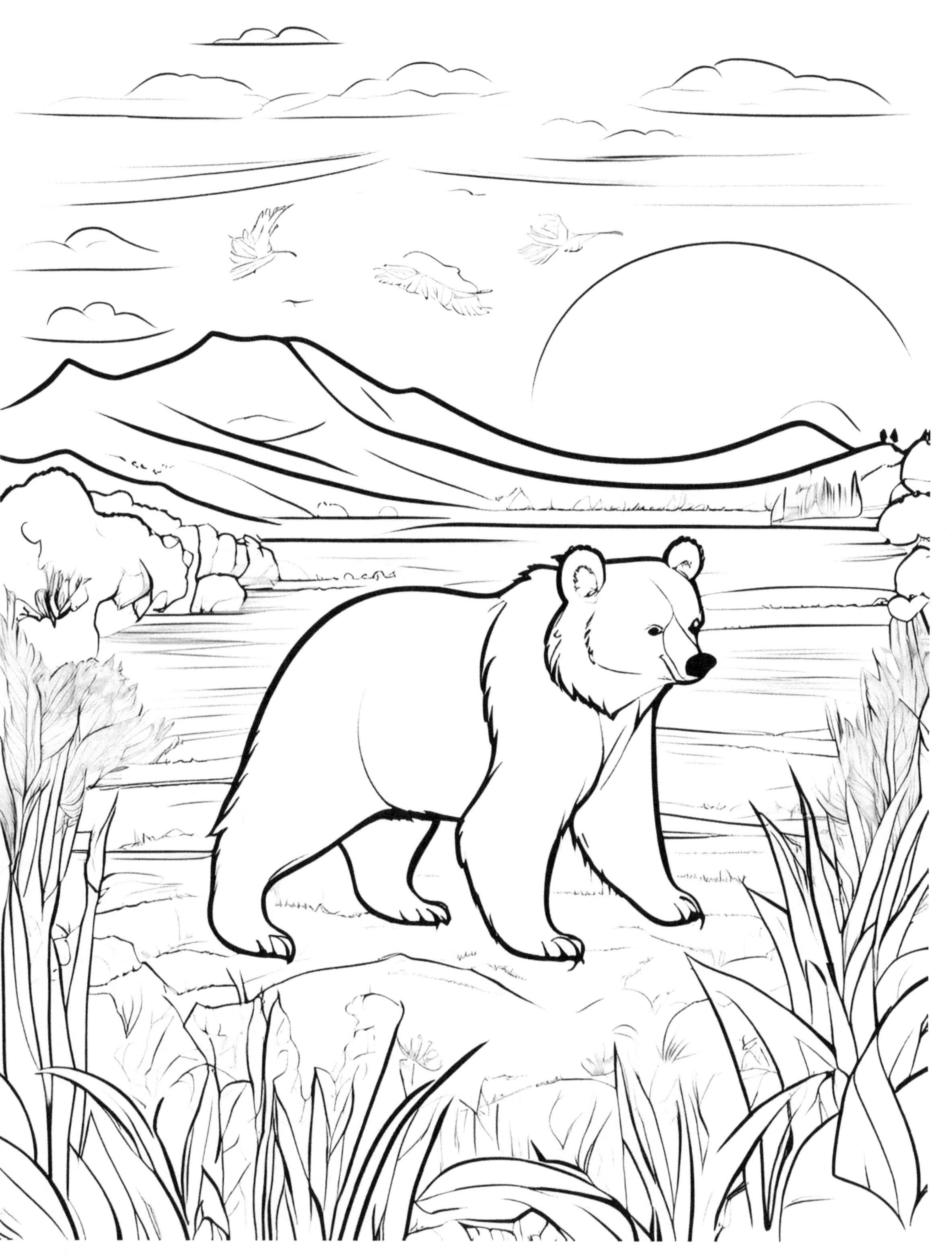

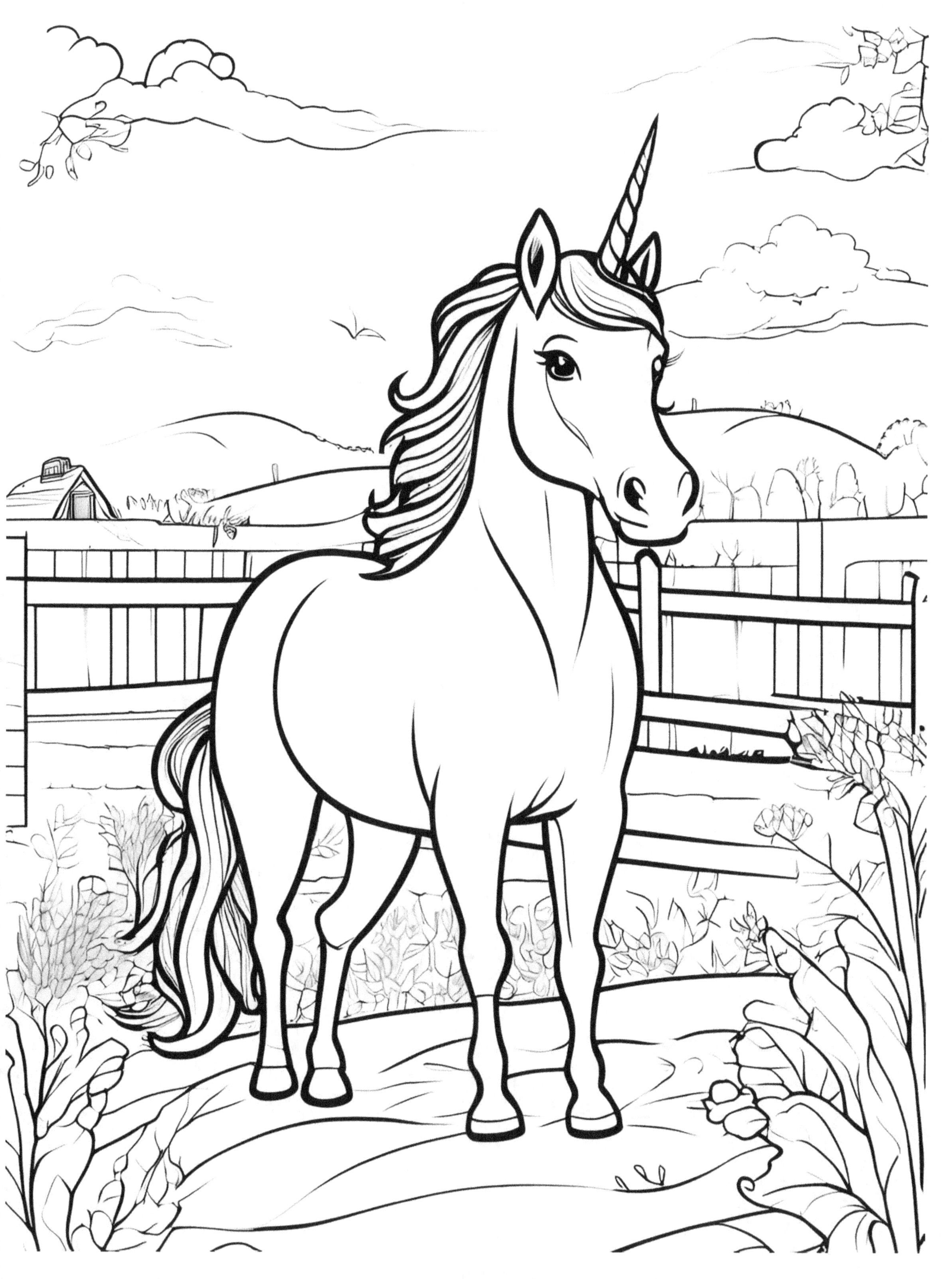

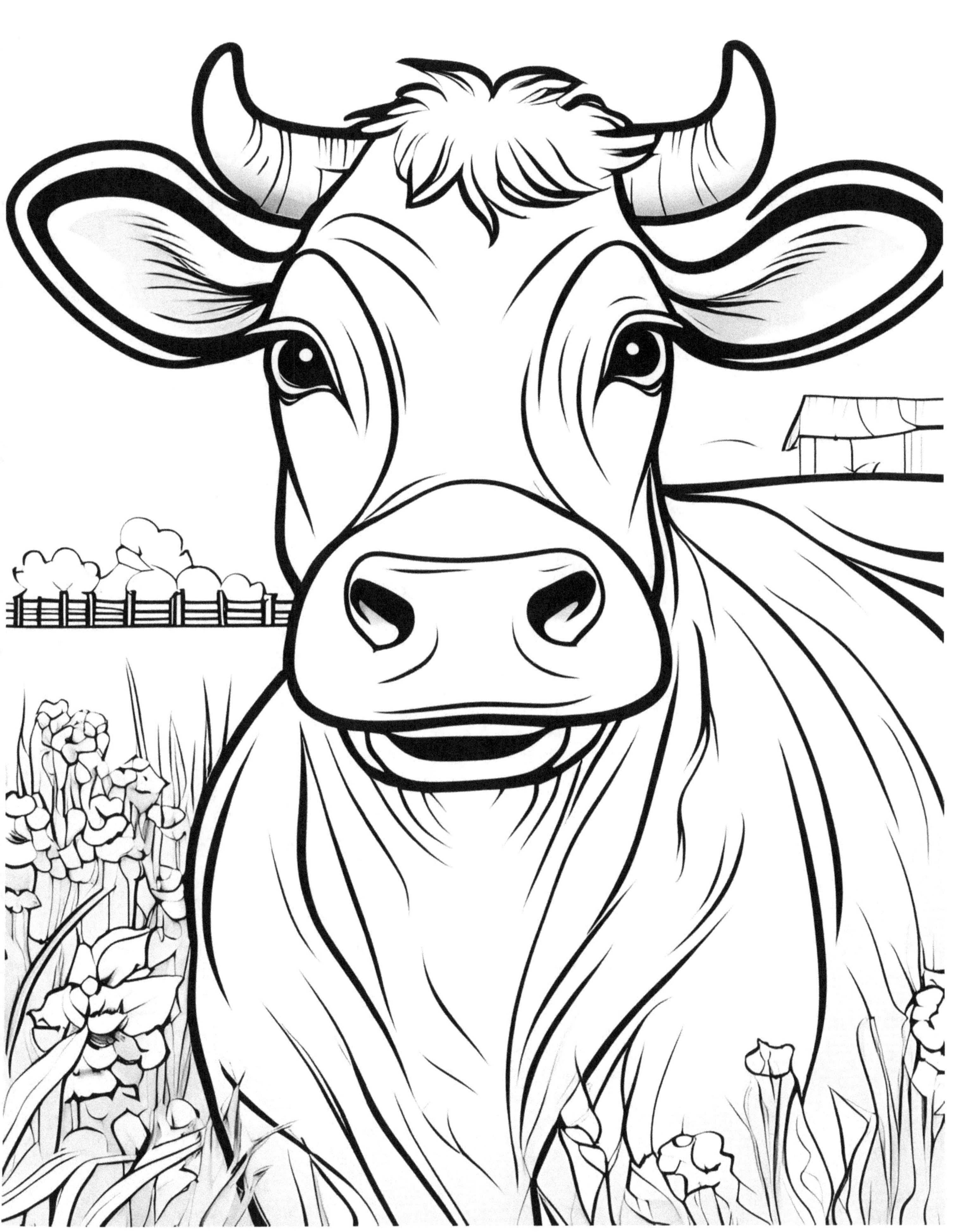

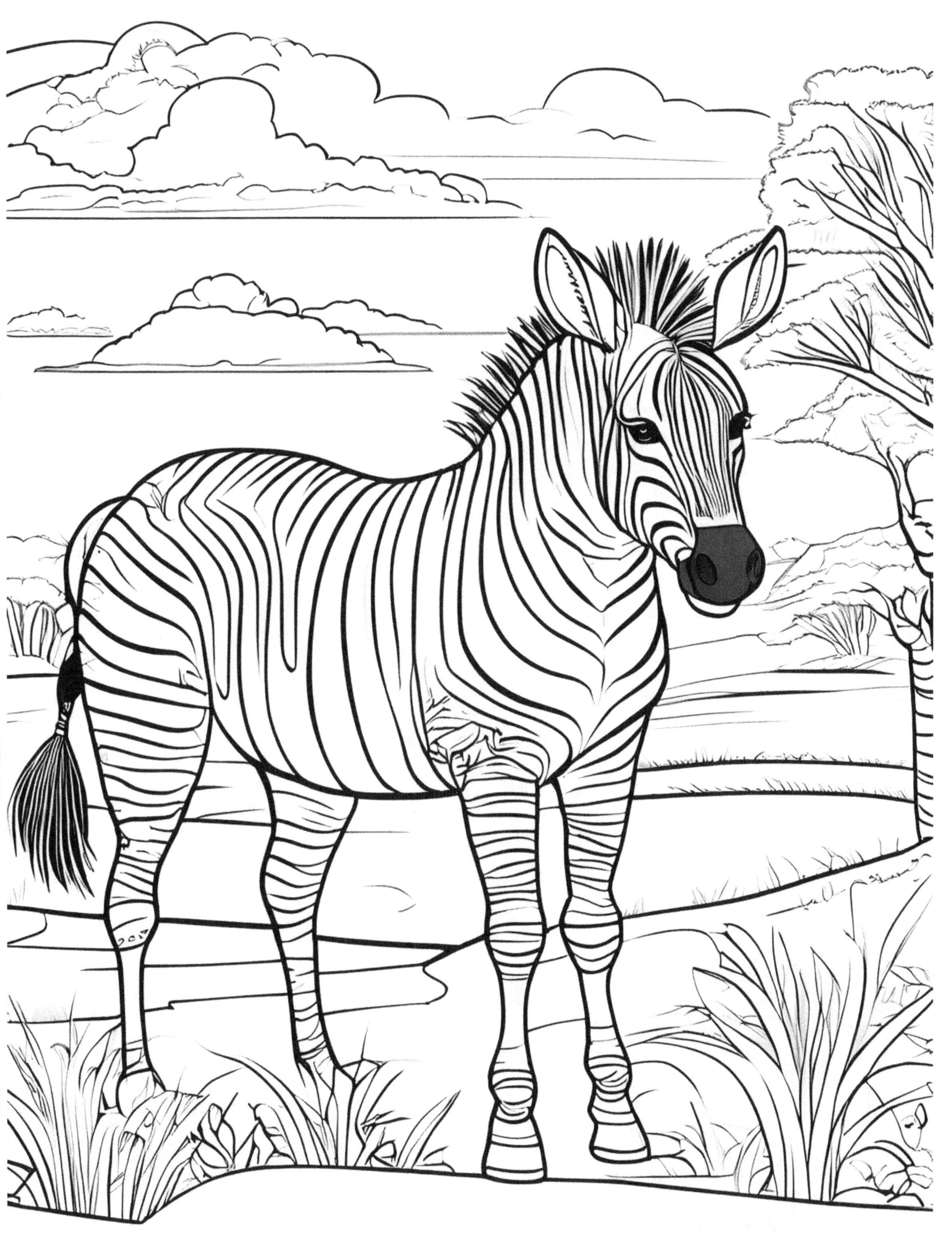